Architectural Gu
New York

A Critic's Guide to 100 Iconic Buildings
in New York from 1999 to 2020

Architectural Guide
New York

A Critic's Guide to 100 Iconic Buildings
in New York from 1999 to 2020

Vladimir Belogolovsky

DOM
publishers

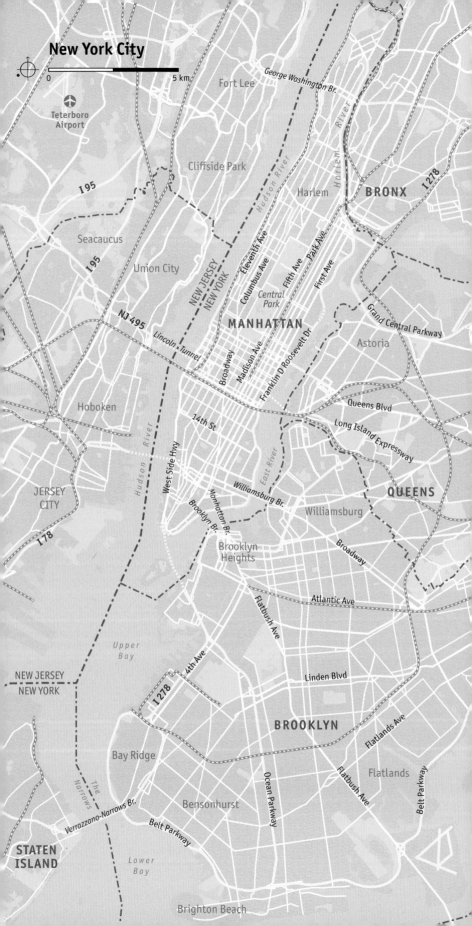

Contents

One World Trade Center. David Childs of SOM, 2013

Iconic New York

Vladimir Belogolovsky

The idea of writing a book about New York City is nothing new, and there is plenty of competition. I've contemplated putting together a new architecture guide for the city for a while, and in the meantime, others have done just that. Yet, our city is so unsettled these days, so stubborn in its obsessive urge to reinvent itself yet again, that the more I waited, the more original, even eccentric structures popped up in its most unexpected and far-reaching corners, and so finally, a new book became irresistible.

What ultimately pushed me to complete this project was a visit to the *Never Built New York* exhibition. Co-curated by Sam Lubell and Greg Goldin, who were also the authors of its namesake book, it opened at the Queens Museum in September 2017. I realized something right then — despite the audacity of the many unrealized structures cited by the authors in their vision of the fantastic ghost-city that could have been, the truth is that New York today presents an even more breathtaking metropolis. Sure, Frank Gehry's Guggenheim in the form of "a frenetic jumble of titanium, concrete, and glass" next to the Brooklyn Bridge or the geometrically adventurous towers by Santiago Calatrava and Moshe Safdie would have made it even more thrilling. Nevertheless, look around — early 21st century New York has risen and it is worth celebrating.

However, as recently as in 1998, Kenneth Frampton, the leading architectural historian and critic shared a peculiar thought. He remarked that one of the most embarrassing aspects for him living in New York City is that, "When people come to New York and ask — 'well, what was built here recently of interest?' You basically can't say anything of what is of interest, whatsoever." He then admitted that a couple of buildings were on the drawing boards and if they were to go ahead, maybe there was some hope. Frampton was referring to the Japanese architect

Yoshio Taniguchi's planned expansion of the Museum of Modern Art, a project which had won an international competition. Another was the late Raimund Abraham's winning design for the Austrian Cultural Forum. Still, the historian expressed his doubts that these works would ever be realized, and even if they were, those would be just two examples of architecture of any note in the sea of ordinary buildings built in New York year after year by profit-driven developers.

Frampton's diagnosis was so somber, who would have thought that not only would those two projects be realized, but at least 100 truly distinctive buildings, exploring every possible program and scale would be built since then, and many more are being planned or are under construction. New York has become a true testing ground for architectural creativity. Moreover, there are so many iconic buildings that have emerged over the last two decades all across the city that already some critics are asking — how many icons do we need?

There is now even resistance to some truly innovative projects for their sheer audacity and otherworldliness. For example, British designer Thomas Heatherwick's 150-foot-tall climbable, pine-cone-like sculpture called *Vessel*, a centerpiece of the Public Square and Gardens that has already topped out at Hudson Yards, was attacked by critics from the day it was made public. It was condemned as expensive, despite being entirely financed by billionaire developer Stephen Ross, and dubbed a "stairway to nowhere." Some critics even went as far as calling it insensitively a suicide platform.

Protests by concerned environmentalists nixed Heatherwick's Pier 55, a park and futuristic events venue that was to jut into the Hudson River near West 13th Street. However, according to the most recent reports this daring project, widely known as "Diller Island" because it was funded by Barry Diller, another billion-aire businessman, is not dead quite yet and has resumed its construction after being halted for one year. It is now being planned to open in 2020 as the centerpiece of the 4.5-mile (7.2-kilometer)-long Hudson River Park.

Even before the 2008 global economic crisis forced numerous projects in the city to be put on hold, the critics advanced their attacks on the most daring and ambitious proposals. Perhaps the most telling example of this outbreak was when the developer-friendly Bloomberg mayoral administration decided to lop 200 feet (61 meters) off the 53 West 53rd Street tower proposed by Parisian architect and Pritzker Prize laureate Jean Nouvel that was originally 1,250 feet (381 meters). This beautifully designed edifice was approved only after the architect scaled down the building's spire, the feature that New York always promoted and celebrated.

Beauty in today's architecture is one topic that critics try to avoid despite the fact that it is obviously one of the main criteria of any masterwork, whether a building, a sculpture, or a painting. Beauty is, of course, subjective. Still, there are some examples that win our hearts right away. Wouldn't the Oculus, the transportation hub built at Ground Zero, qualify as such? Yet, the critics hesitate to admit its merits. Designed by Santiago Calatrava, the New York-based Spanish architect, engineer, sculptor, and painter, the structure is arguably the most iconic building in New York since the Twin Towers, the original World Trade Center. It is now our most photographed space. But because critics are uncomfortable with its price tag, they ask how many other ordinary, but much more needed structures could have been built instead? What a shortsighted view! It is so essential for New York or any other city to have extraordinary civic structures and spaces in addition to, and not instead of, much-needed infrastructure and other public works. Both are required to make the city not only more convenient, efficient, and safe, but also more delightful, enjoyable, noble, and ultimately a more beautiful place, the kind of place where its citizens are proud to live and share with the world.

Plenty of great buildings planned for the city never materialized. That is the nature of architecture, and the *Never Built New York* book and exhibition put many of these unrealized dreams in perspective. But what is particularly disheartening here is how many buildings were built throughout the city's history only to be ruthlessly taken down. So often, these were our best buildings. And after we lost such irreplaceable landmarks as the Singer Building (1908–1968), Pennsylvania Station (1910–1963), and numerous dazzling mansions built for the city's wealthiest families along Fifth Avenue during the Gilded Age, one would have hoped we had learned something.

Not us, though, so this greedy destruction is an ongoing affair and, as recently as in 2014, the world-class American Folk Art Museum, which won plenty of awards, including Best Public Cultural Building in the World, and Best New Building in the World in 2002 by *World Architecture* magazine, was shamelessly demolished by none other than its next-door neighbor, the most-celebrated Museum of Modern Art, for yet another aggressive expansion. "We don't collect buildings and we don't collect them for a reason," said MoMA's director Glenn D. Lowry, authoritatively announcing the demolition verdict. Before the building was turned into dust its most distinctive feature, the folded white-bronze facade, was put into storage. As it turns out, MoMA does collect buildings, although not in one piece. Will the facade be eventually put on display there? What will the storyline reveal about this prominent but awkward acquisition?

The building was designed by locals Tod Williams and Billie Tsien, architects also known for their beautifully crafted Barnes Foundation in Philadelphia and Barack Obama's Presidential library and museum in Chicago, now in planning. Their American Folk Art Museum building lasted for just 13 years. New York continues to live up to its name in a most unsentimental way.

Ironically, Diller Scofidio + Renfro, the architects brought in by MoMA to remove the short-lived Folk Art building's corpse, and to install their own new wing for the Museum, are among our best designers responsible for the most talked

432 Park Avenue. Rafael Viñoly, 2016

"Successful experimental buildings should be celebrated as extraordinary achievements. If we don't recognize that, it is the end of our profession."

Thom Mayne, in a 2016 interview with the author

about projects in recent history, including the High Line Park, the Lincoln Center redevelopment, and The Shed, a new experimental cultural institution in Hudson Yards, soon to be completed.

And so, here goes New York's familiar story of perpetual growth: we don't conserve, expand, or build next to something that has already taken root, instead we uproot and replace the existing buildings entirely, or in some rare cases build right on top, such as in the cases of the Hearst Tower by British architect Norman Foster or The Porter House by SHoP. Something must give, while one only hopes that an even greater architecture can be achieved in this stern process.

Iconic Buildings

Now, let us examine what constitutes the iconic. Why do we need these icons and why celebrate them in this book? What do they do for our city? As in any discipline, architecture accumulates its most distinctive creations. Of course, the term "iconic" is somewhat exaggerated. Only a fraction of the buildings selected for this book can be identified as true icons. These are the works that stand out from their context, and turn our interaction with the city and other citizens into a meaningful, pleasant, and stimulating urban experience. An icon may be a memorable image, representative of its time and place, as well as

its architect's aspirations. It also helps us orient ourselves. The Empire State Building and the Chrysler Building are such cases. While the former points to the very center of New York, where Fifth Avenue and 34th Street cross, the latter marks the location of the Grand Central Station. Another example of an icon is something people can engage with directly, such as that magical street in the sky, Brooklyn Bridge, with its characteristic interlaced steel cables slicing New York's skyline into a myriad of accidental trapezoids and triangles. To be sure, an iconic building is a work of art by a talented artist, an emotional gesture embraced and loved by people.

Over the last two decades numerous icons have been added to our city. One could even say New York is a different city now. Yet, I would argue that we still need more such creations here, because if we ask New Yorkers to name iconic landmarks in the city, chances are, most would refer to structures built dozens of years ago, if not more than a century. Think of the Statue of Liberty, Trinity Church, Grand Central Station, the Woolworth Building, the Flatiron Building, Rockefeller Center, the Waldorf Astoria, or among more recent examples — the Guggenheim, the Seagram Building, and the Verrazzano-Narrows Bridge.

The Twin Towers, for sure, were the city's most powerful modern icon. Portrayed on television and in films, these buildings were not just familiar to people all

View from Midtown, with the Empire State Building in the foreground

around the world, they stood as the embodiment of American capitalism and global power. But buildings built in the 21st century have not risen to the same level of significance in the consciousness of most New Yorkers, let alone the world. Let's be frank: this city, despite its name and quest for non-stop renewal, is not associated with the contemporary moment. Yet, in the last two decades, so many innovative buildings that try so very hard to be iconic have been added. Every city block competes for attention. It is perhaps the most thrilling time to be here, ever. The city is certainly renewing itself once again on an epic scale, if not in terms of modernizing its crumbling infrastructure, then at least as far as its urban and architectural image is concerned.

In a 2008 interview, I asked Vienna-based architect Wolf Prix if he minds it when people compare his truly iconic buildings to insects, wings, hurricanes, or acts of violence. He responded, "I like it. It is not intentional, but what is intentional is that we want to make identifiable and readable buildings. I love it when people give buildings nicknames. A city, in order to be experienced, must be describable, meaning it should feature identifiable and iconic buildings. As an architect I want people to remember my buildings. That's all." As the author of this guide I want people to note which 100 buildings I think are iconic. To help with remembering these buildings I have given them nicknames. My readers may agree or disagree, or they may come up with their own analogies, which I encourage.

New York is a city on the water; four of its five boroughs are either islands or parts of islands with a total coastline of 578 miles (930 kilometers). Until recently this was one of the city's best-kept secrets. Today, thanks to the leadership of its three-term mayor Michael Bloomberg, New York is a humane green city of promenades and parks, many of which lined our formerly inaccessible shores. Bloomberg also created the innovative Design and Construction Excellence initiative, based on the U.S. General Services Administration's Design Excellence program, which aims to improve the city's public buildings by inviting the most talented designers, chosen on a competitive basis, to design public buildings. It was also during his administration that Janette Sadik-Khan, then New York City Transportation Commissioner, led urban redevelopment by taking traffic lanes away

Cooper Union Academic Building. Thom Mayne of Morphosis with Gruzen Samton, 2009

Photo: Alex Fradkin

from cars and giving them to pedestrians, bikes, and buses, thus reclaiming hundreds of acres of urban space and making it easier for people to get around. Her recent *Street Fight: Handbook for an Urban Revolution*, now serves as an empowering roadmap for rethinking and reinvigorating cities around the world. She said, "If you can change the street, you can change the world." So true and so effective. It is also worth mentioning the new ferry services our current mayor Bill de Blasio initiated. These handsome speedy boats now crisscross New York Harbor for the cost of a subway ride. End-to-end, their routes span over 60 miles of waterway.

Photo: Evan Joseph

Mercedes House. Enrique Norten of Ten Arquitectos, 2012

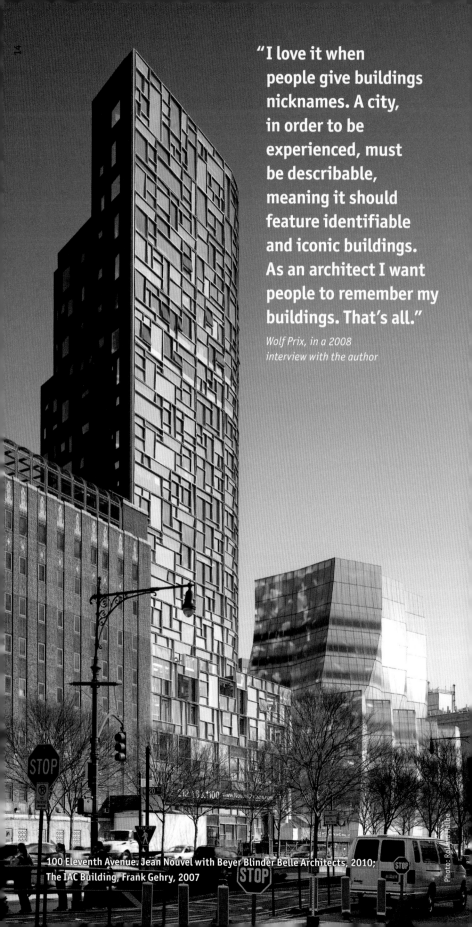

"I love it when people give buildings nicknames. A city, in order to be experienced, must be describable, meaning it should feature identifiable and iconic buildings. As an architect I want people to remember my buildings. That's all."

Wolf Prix, in a 2008 interview with the author

100 Eleventh Avenue. Jean Nouvel with Beyer Blinder Belle Architects, 2010; The IAC Building, Frank Gehry, 2007

Photo: Roland Halbe

This Book's Mission

The mission of this book is to document and celebrate New York's transformative energy by gathering one hundred of the most iconic buildings built since 1999, a date whose significance I will explain later in this text. The list includes some structures that are still under construction and will be finished within the next couple of years. The period in question is representative of architectural developments both locally and globally, and in fact, most of the selected buildings were designed either by foreign architects or those who settled here and now call New York home; I particularly wanted to indicate all of the featured architects' origins to stress this point. It is during this span of time in architecture when the originality and signature-style authorship of architects as artists was encouraged and celebrated by the media, professional critics, and, of course, their clients. This type of artistic architecture is no longer appreciated by critics and downplayed by architects themselves, which is a strong indication that the book's period will stand out as distinctively eccentric.

Ever since Frank Gehry's Guggenheim Museum was built in Bilbao, Spain, in 1997, the architecture of so many major cultural institutions around the world was aimed at building a visual spectacle. There is a wonderful aphorism by philosopher Walter Benjamin, "Architecture is mostly appreciated by an ordinary person in a state of distraction." Distraction Bilbao delivered in full. But more than that, Gehry's building turned around the depressed economy of the entire Basque region.

The "Bilbao Effect" followed: mayors, multinational corporations, university presidents, museum directors, and the super rich all over the globe soon appropriated iconic architecture for its marketing value and as a way to spur economic development. The new trend played well into the architects' common psyche. For years, our leading design schools had been pushing architects' originality to the max. In one of his last interviews, prominent Italian critic Manfredo Tafuri (1935–1994) said: "Today architects are forced into either being a star or being a nobody." And in my own 2016 interview with Thom Mayne, the Pritzker Prize-winning Los Angeles-based architect who now maintains a busy New York office, responded to a question about his search for a personal and distinguished voice by confessing something quite remarkable: "I asked myself, 'Who am I? How can I participate in this collaboration of voices?' It was not ego, it was the fear of being nothing."

Another important milestone that needs to be mentioned here is December 18, 2002, when the world's leading architects presented their semifinalist schemes for the redevelopment of Ground Zero. The attention to their post-9/11 proposals to redefine New York's skyline and reaffirm its identity as the financial and cultural capital of the Western world was global, live, and in primetime. Architecture became front page news. Shortly thereafter, the leading architects were featured as guests on popular TV shows and they started being routinely referred to as starchitects. Their designs grew in extravagance, while professional criticism was quickly replaced by praise and advertising. The "iconic" became the norm and was in high demand. Architecture was now advertised as art, which helped to drive real estate prices to never-before-seen heights. In some parts of the world, entire developments were named after their architects. All bets were on the stars, their talents, charisma, and their ability to turn mere buildings into masterworks of architecture. This run of highly original, iconic buildings all over the world was challenged by Beijing's CCTV Headquarters (2012) designed by Dutch starchitect Rem Koolhaas, who is also the author of *Delirious New York* (1978) and founder of the Rotterdam based office OMA, with its New York branch recently commissioned for the expansion of New York's New Museum, which is still at too early a stage of design to be included in this book. The CCTV was conceived as a twisted loop to produce the most original building there, rather than merely being the tallest. The premise was that the status of the tallest building in a particular city, or even in the entire world, can only be kept temporarily. But a building of great originality would always stand out.

But All That Originality Couldn't Last

However, the trend for creating original buildings proved to be just another fad, and was abruptly put to the test by the 2008 world financial crisis, which started on Wall Street and deepened with the collapse of the Lehman Brothers, a global financial powerhouse and fourth-largest investment bank in the U.S. that happened to have been headquartered in Manhattan. Despite the seriousness of the crisis, just a few years later all the losses were turned into gains, as the Dow Jones was breaking new records at a higher and higher pace. Still, despite the economy's robust rebound, pure form-making in architecture had by then lost its momentum. Even if budgets may allow, it is now no longer considered ethical to indulge in architecture as personalized art form. Now so many of our leading architects' most daring projects are being scrutinized by critics who, for the most part, demonstrate their utter confusion at the still ongoing but quickly fading proliferation of personalized styles. There are so many ways of making architecture that we no longer seem to know or even care about a difference between good, excellent, or plain mediocre. There are no longer authorities or so-called taste-setters. Is there anyone who we can trust unconditionally? Any critic can condemn anything that's spectacular and justify anything that's boring, while architects can reject any criticism by replying playfully, "but why not?" Their reasoning for doing what they do can be celebrated to a point, but it has become questionable, to say the least.

For example, here is how New York-based architect Robert Stern, the Dean of Yale University's Architecture School from 1998 to 2016, described some of the reasoning behind his architecture in our 2012 interview: "There is a difference of approach, depending on the project, where it is, my mood, what I had for breakfast, what new book came across my desk..." Clearly, architects have lost their grounding. The idea that architecture is art and they are true artists performing on a grand urban scale has clouded their real intentions. In fact, very few can state them clearly. Ask them — What is architecture? And most will be caught off guard, and will not produce a meaningful response. Believe me, I've tried! Again, it was Koolhaas

MoMA addition. Yoshio Taniguchi with KPF, 2004

Photo: Courtesy of The Museum of Modern Art

Hearst Tower. Foster + Partners, 2006

who offered his diagnosis of the profession in his interview with German journalist Hanno Rauterberg, in his 2008 book *Talking Architecture*. He said, "I think what we are experiencing is the global triumph of eccentricity. Lots of extravagant buildings are being built, buildings that have no meaning, no functionality. It's rather about spectacular shapes and, of course, the architects' egos."

Now having heard from some of the architects, should we blame critics for not being critical? Presently, it comes down to my opinion being just as good as yours. Architectural criticism has lost its meaning and relevance. We are going through a period in architecture in which any architect can be awarded the discipline's most coveted prize and the lamest project can land on the cover of any leading professional magazine. Follow the professional press and you will quickly realize that there are no longer tendencies, movements, or even serious discussions on theories, aesthetics, or such essential aspects of architecture as form-making.

Decisions to publish one project over another are driven either by personal agendas, friendships, favoritism, or are completely random. How can critics be objective these days? Few are left because the public is more interested in reading about travel or real estate than they are in architecture. More than one rushed to the sides of the architects they once criticized to represent them as their PR managers. To be fair, what choice did they have? In any case, having so many critics questioning whether it was a good thing for architects to create architecture that is novel for novelty's sake alone, may not have been a bad thing after all.

Eventually, too many architects having too many ideas reached a saturation point and triggered a need for them to find some form of commonality among themselves. The absence of professional criticism does not mean that architecture is not a critical profession, so self-criticism eventually formed from within. "Common Ground" was chosen as a theme of the 2012 Venice Architecture Biennale, the profession's most prestigious global forum. At the time, common ground was the last thing architects wanted. But since the question was posed by the Biennale's director, British architect David Chipperfield, the idea found traction, particularly among the young architects who had given in to so much pressure for originality.

They were at least reassured by Koolhaas' refusal to continue creating original,

Columbia University Medical Center.
Diller Scofidio + Renfro with Gensler, 2016

iconic buildings after realizing that his CCTV gesture had topped them all. He publicly admitted that he was no longer interested in that game. It was then that architects' focus has shifted from stylizing buildings as objects to creating socially engaging and ecologically sustainable environments. Saving the environment had been on architects' minds for a while; now it became a much broader movement. Still, planting a few trees here and there or the use of sustainable materials and techniques, did not sound quite exciting enough to proclaim a new paradigm shift in the discipline.

A New Identity Crisis?

By 2014, the profession reached its deepest identity crisis in modern times and it seemed that only Koolhaas himself could point to the right direction, as he was asked to be the director of the Venice Biennale that year. He grabbed the opportunity to emphasize the seriousness of the situation, but instead of proposing his new vision he decided to break every thing apart into so-called fundamental elements of architecture; he called his biennale, "Fundamentals." Shortly after the Biennale I discussed its significance and consequences with another starchitect, New York-based Peter Eisenman, who offered his take on his former student's exhibition, "Rem's Biennale was like a trade show, a catalog, Internet shopping... The Biennale was not about ideas and how these elements go together. Architecture should not be about its parts, but the syntax. Architecture is about putting things together."

Photo: Alexander Severin

837 Washington. Morris Adjmi of MA, 2014

The confusion lasted for another two years until the 2016 Venice Biennale's new director, Chilean architect Alejandro Aravena, who had just been named that year's Pritzker Prize winner. He finally pinpointed contemporary architecture's *raison d'etre*. He titled his Biennale "Re porting from the Front." In his own en trance pavilion, he arranged over 90 tons of waste (7 miles [11 km] of scrap metal and 10,000 sqm of plasterboard) left over from the previous year's Art Biennale. The message — the common ground that architects were desperately looking for — was finally identified as problem-solving. In other words, let's not dream up some unrealistic projects for a few elite clients but stick to the real problems, of which the world has plenty.

When interviewing Aravena in his office in Santiago, Chile, in 2014, I asked him to comment on a remark Wolf Prix made to me, which was, "My students learn to shape their ideas not conditioned by the reality of constraints and clichés but by the reality of possibilities." Aravena was highly critical of this view and dismissed everything that is not directed at problem-solving as arbitrary and meaningless.

He told me, "I am doing architecture for a reason. I want to build projects better than they were done be fore. Not just different, but better. Better, meaning not just as far as design, but better in terms of the living conditions." This directness resonated with many architects and out of many voices it was the priority of problem-solving that is now on everyone's lips. The priorities have shifted from the quest to discover unique solo identities and voices to a teamwork approach, and to solving pragmatic issues at hand. Architects, particularly the younger generation, now praise themselves for refusing to attach to their architecture any kind of personal authorship. Bjarke Ingels, the Copenhagen and New York-based starchitect told me in our 2009 interview, "Our architecture is never triggered by a single event, never conceived by a single mind, and never shaped by a single hand. Neither is it the direct materialization of a personal agenda or pure ideals, but rather the result of an ongoing adaptation to the multiple conflicting forces flowing through society."

Really? Wasn't architecture always about "the multiple conflicting forces

Photo: William Paterson

The IAC Building. Frank Gehry, 2007

flowing through society?" Sure, but now it is problem-solving that is elevated above everything else. Comparing architecture to art became a dangerous thought. Very few old-school architects still believe that openly. Most of our younger architects shy away from defining their craft as art or admitting being inspired by a particular vision or an image; such views are no longer celebrated. The architects' designs are now more like spreadsheets of calculations rationalizing every spike and twist. Everything willful and artistic is carefully removed from being even mentioned. Absolutely every step of the design process is defended as logical, consequential, or even inevitable.

Architecture turned into the direct response to the site, context, sun angles, views, program, budget, and so on. Personal agendas tend to be completely suppressed now so as not to distract clients, or annoy critics who may condemn a particular project that shows just about any sign of artistry as expensive, wasteful, or even unethical. Lately I wonder whether I should take a break for a few years from interviewing architects because their responses, whether we meet in New York,

Beijing, Moscow, or Mexico City are becoming suspiciously similar.

One of the things I always ask architects is what single words or phrases best describe their work. The range of answers has been vast, and even as recently as five years ago I never heard the same term mentioned twice. I repeat, never. Here are just a few examples: "aligned precision," "misalignments," "complexities," "deep structure," "self-referential," "notion of randomness," "clarity," "pursuit of ambiguity," "incomplete," "provocative," "fun," "speed," and "forget gravity!" When I ask the same question now, whether I am in China, Australia, Mexico, Japan, or Russia, the answer is consistent and singular. The first word I hear almost every single time is this: "nature." At least as far as our leading architects are concerned, the transition from recently egocentric and form-driven architecture to eco-centric or earth-centric is now complete.

If you wonder, how long will it take before our leading architects' buildings will start reflecting what they are actually saying, the answer is this — these generically packaged, lookalike buildings have already arrived. There are buildings in Manhattan by such superstars as Tadao Ando, David Chipperfied, Norman Foster, Herzog & de Meuron, Richard Meier, Renzo Piano, Richard Rogers, and Rafael Viñoly that have not even a hint of who may have designed them; we no longer can be entirely certain. Are we facing generic and identity-stripped architecture even from our leading architects? This is no longer a rhetorical question because what is upon us is a matter-of-fact identity crisis, and now, looking back to 2012, when Chipperfield challenged architects with finding common ground among them, should be identified as the peak of creativity. Then one thing that was common was speaking of the importance of self-identity in architecture. When will the architects become brave enough again not to care about what their potential critics may think?

One only hopes that this state of architectural affairs is a temporary retreat because as another very wise Bologna and New York-based architect, Emilio Ambasz, put it, "The real task of architecture begins once functional and behavioral needs have been satisfied. It is not hunger, but love and fear — and sometimes wonder — which make us create. The architect's cultural and social context changes constantly, but his task remains always the same: to give poetic form to the pragmatic." Another local architect, Ric Scofidio addressed the issue of problem-solving in a more direct way in our conversation in 2017. He said, "I find that problem-solving alone can become so pragmatic and deadly for architecture because it should be all about questioning. And maybe the first question to ask should be whether the problem at hand should be solved at all or is it enough? To me problem-solving is too limiting and not interesting. Architecture was never just about that. Making problems is more fun; solving problems is too easy."

When Did the Iconic Period Start and Is It Over?

Architecture is a fascinating discipline. While good architecture may be about creating a balance between the pragmatic and the poetic, great architecture is entirely something else. It is all about breaking with any kind of balance, conventions, or even common sense for that matter. Should architects aim for being good or great? Perhaps both would be the appropriate answer. In any case, I see the current state of architectural affairs as something quite positive because architects now question what they do with greater scrutiny and more doors have opened up to so many more architects who could never dream about being at the forefront of the profession.

Now they can publish their work more widely and compete with the profession's leaders and even win, as pure originality is no longer the only consideration for success. The playing field has become literally flat and anyone can get ahead, at

One57. Christian de Portzamparc, 2014

"Cities depend on very strong gestures."

Rafael Viñoly, in a 2007 interview with the author

HL23, as seen from the High Line.
Neil Denari Architects with Marc Rosenbaum Architects, 2012

Photo: Courtesy of Neil Denari Architects

least for now. Inevitably, personified, expressionistic architecture will be watered down, and here in New York this means one thing with certainty: the group of buildings built during the period this guide puts together will stand out as one of the most distinctive chapters in the city's architectural history.

On a personal level I must add that the task of identifying 100 structures for this guide is very dear to me, not only because I remember how these buildings were first imagined, debated, and finally realized, but also because I remember the time when nothing was going up in New York at all. In the early and mid-1990s the city's building activity was practically nonexistent and just a few very boring structures, seemingly unwillingly, were advancing up ever so slowly. All that changed by the end of that decade, and then came the threshold year: 1999.

LVMH Tower. Christian de Portzamparc, 1999

Photo: Nicolas Borel

Something was in the air because suddenly, several new buildings were making headlines. There were gill-like metal screens dancing around the open-air exit stairs in the back of the Korean Presbyterian Church in Sunnyside, Queens, designed by a pioneering parametrics trio Douglas Garofalo, Greg Lynn, and Michael McInturf. There was a discussion about multistory switchback ramps with precision, high-tech articulation behind expansive glass facade of the Lerner Hall Student Center by Bernard Tschumi at Columbia University.

And, finally, in the very heart of Manhattan's luxury shopping district, along East 57th Street near Madison Avenue, the 24-story LVMH Tower, with its elegant, multicolored, flower-inspired glass facade designed by the Pritzker Prize-winning Parisian architect Christian de Portzamparc, attracted praise when it opened in December that year. It was heralded as the best new building in New York in a generation. As a group, these novel buildings signaled the city's reawakening interest in architecture as an art form. These early built examples and a number of then-planned buildings were absolutely startling because there were so few of them, and the change was nothing short of groundbreaking and radical.

In fact, to mention anything of note built in New York before the late '90s, one would have to go as far back as mid-1980s when the AT&T Building and the Lipstick Building were added to our skyline. Designed by Philip Johnson and John Burgee, they took then-popular Postmodernism to a new, urban scale. Before that, the last significant works of architecture in New York were the iconic Citicorp Center (1977) designed by Hugh Stubbins, and the Twin Towers (1976) of the World Trade Center by Japanese-American architect Minoru Yamasaki. And prior to that, the most significant architectural buildings in New York were built back in the 1960s, notably the Ford Foundation (1968) on East 42nd Street designed by Kevin Roche, and One Chase Manhattan Plaza, now 28 Liberty Street (1964), by Gordon Bunshaft of Skidmore, Owings & Merrill. Recalling this context, it is now easier to understand the significance of the above-mentioned buildings that arrived here in 1999, and which opened a way for many adventurous projects that were to be built soon afterwards.

My subjective list of buildings includes 100 works. To be sure, I could have easily added another 20 or so buildings, but I prefer to have less than more. Sometimes a particular building with a stronger identity won out over a better project, as far as its architectural aspects; other times the decision was based on the availability of more effective images versus the ones that I would need to take myself or settle with the ones offered by architects who

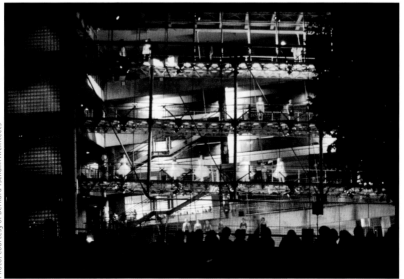

Photo: Courtesy of Bernard Tschumi Architects

Lerner Hall Student Center. Bernard Tschumi with Gruzen Samton Architects, 1999

Photo: Danny Bright

Carroll House, East Williamsburg, Brooklyn. LOT-EK, 2016.

are less concerned with their creations' representations. I also decided not to feature interiors here, as I think they deserve a separate publication. Of course, there are a few projects on my list where you can't quite separate the two.

There are no single-family, freestanding houses on my list, except one built in 2016 in East Williamsburg, Brooklyn, by LOT-EK. By including just this one house, I wanted to emphasize the ultraconservative tastes of New Yorkers for this type of construction. In fact, the city did not produce a single Modernist or Postmodernist house. One can travel across the Five Boroughs all day long and not find a single house that even remotely evokes progress and innovation. By and large, houses built here in the last decade or so look like they are products of the 19th century. Apparently, LOT-EK were the first architects in the history of New York who asked a simple question: What is or may be a contemporary house? It is puzzling to me that out of tens of thousands of New York-based architects none came to this basic revelation — if I can't find a client to build an innovative house I will build one for myself to set an example! Unlike their counterparts in other cities New York architects prefer to live anonymously behind generic facades.

City of Many Futures

Glancing over the selected buildings, as well as New York's total building stock, this multilayered city is surely one of the most fascinating building projects in history. It is not because it is distinguished by cohesive urban ensembles, or because of the beauty of its individual buildings, or its efficient connectivity. It is because more than any other city in the world, it is not intended to be ever completed or to reflect a particular idealistic vision, unlike such places as Paris, Washington D.C., Saint Petersburg, or Brasilia to name just a few of world's most beautiful cities. New York is conceived as a work in progress. Its compact, repetitive street grid, pragmatically put together of straight lines, right angles, and diligently numbered, ensures that there will never be one dominant center. There is no hierarchy, just relentless accumulation. Any one of the city's many thousands of identical blocks may become its new center, and there is no guarantee that it will stay that way for long. Manhattan's island typography will push up its already mind-boggling density, and its growth upwards will continue to advance, while the greedy nature of its inhabitants will assure constant and unsentimental renewal. New York is an open-ended city in a perpetual state of becoming. In a way, New York is a city of many futures.

My memory of coming to New York 29 years ago is forever vivid. Descending seemingly right over the Twin Towers, then the tallest buildings in the world; landing in a Pan Am Boeing 747 at JFK's TWA Terminal, in its own right the icon of the Jet Age by Eero Saarinen; marching joyfully on its red carpet, while gazing at stylish double-curves of floors turning into ceilings, and finally, discharging to the street, overwhelmed by all kinds of people and the endless queues of stretch limos. A long, long ride at a crawling pace along spaghetti-like highways through never heard of before QUEENS. And suddenly, we were on the old Kosciuszko Bridge, recently blown up and replaced. The view west toward Manhattan was magical. The mirage-like giant metropolis with the most striking sunset in the background, a shimmering vision of impossibly tall buildings lined up from left to right as wide as the horizon. I recall how impatient I was to finally cross the mighty East River. We dove into the Midtown Tunnel and the rest is history. What could be a better place to start afresh for someone at the promising age of 19?!

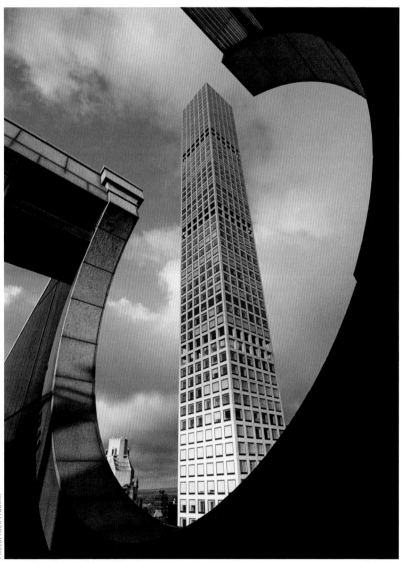

432 Park Avenue. Rafael Viñoly, 2016. Seen here through the broken pediment of the AT&T Building (now named 550 Madison Avenue).

List of Icons

Numbers indicate the project number;
nicknames are on the right-hand side

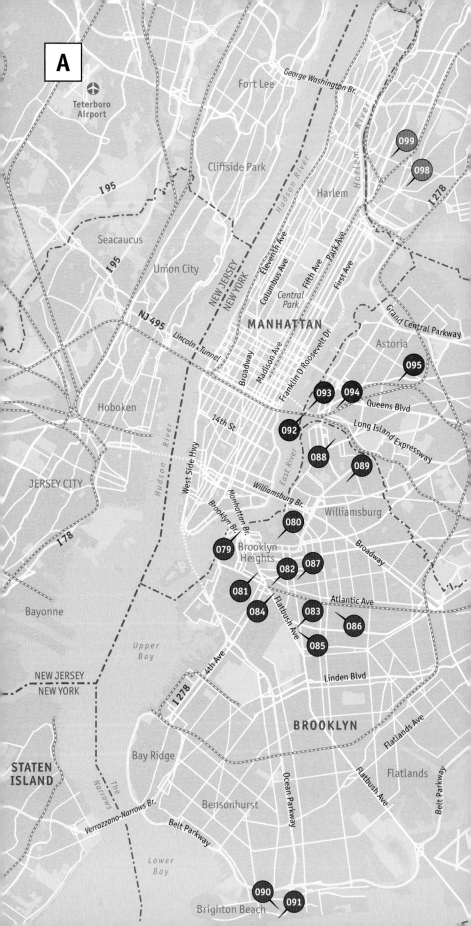

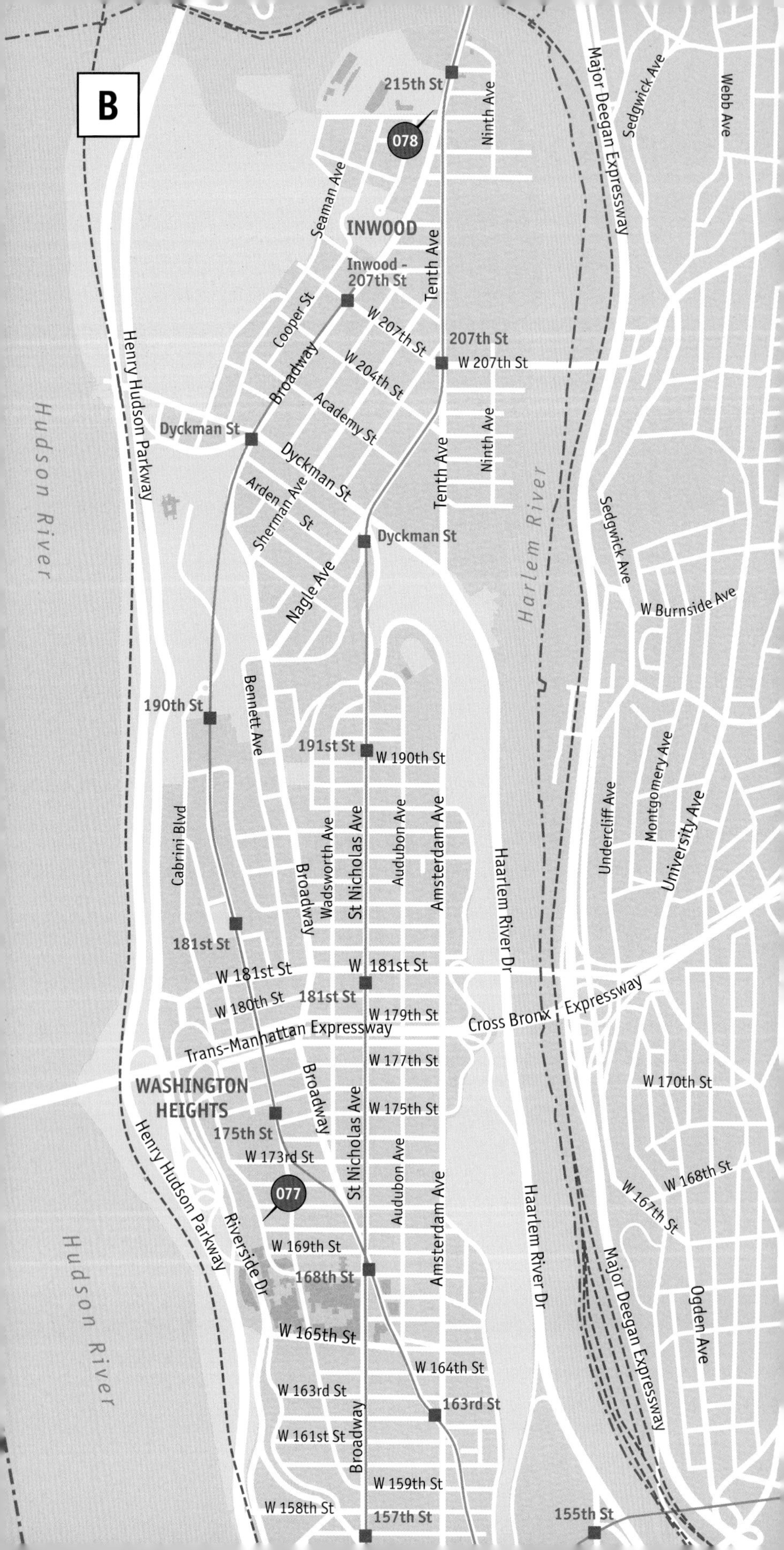

B

215th St
078

Ninth Ave

Seaman Ave

INWOOD

Inwood -
207th St

Tenth Ave

Cooper St

W 207th St

207th St
W 207th St

Broadway

W 204th St

Ninth Ave

Academy St

Dyckman St

Dyckman St

Tenth Ave

Arden Ave
St

Sherman Ave

Dyckman St

Nagle Ave

Harlem River

W Burnside Ave

Sedgwick Ave

Hudson River

Henry Hudson Parkway

190th St

Bennett Ave

191st St
W 190th St

Undercliff Ave

Montgomery Ave

University Ave

Cabrini Blvd

Broadway

Wadsworth Ave

St Nicholas Ave

Audubon Ave

Amsterdam Ave

Haarlem River Dr

181st St

W 181st St
W 180th St

W 181st St
181st St

W 179th St

Cross Bronx Expressway

W 170th St

Trans-Manhattan Expressway

W 177th St

**WASHINGTON
HEIGHTS**

Broadway

W 175th St

175th St
W 173rd St

St Nicholas Ave

Audubon Ave

W 168th St

W 167th St

077

W 169th St

Henry Hudson Parkway

Riverside Dr

168th St

Amsterdam Ave

Haarlem River Dr

Major Deegan Expressway

Ogden Ave

W 165th St

Hudson River

W 164th St

W 163rd St
163rd St

W 161st St

Broadway

W 159th St

155th St

W 158th St
157th St

Sedgwick Ave

Webb Ave

Major Deegan Expressway

Manhattan in Detail

0   1 km

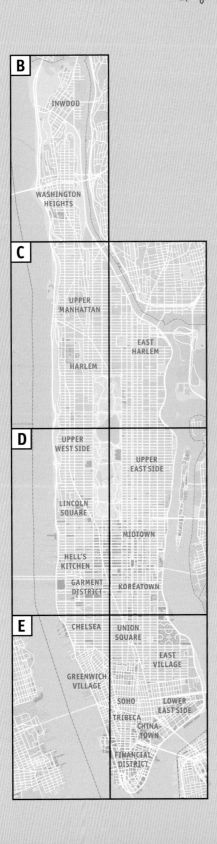

B

INWOOD

WASHINGTON
HEIGHTS

C

UPPER
MANHATTAN

EAST
HARLEM

HARLEM

D

UPPER
WEST SIDE

UPPER
EAST SIDE

LINCOLN
SQUARE

MIDTOWN

HELL'S
KITCHEN

GARMENT
DISTRICT

KOREATOWN

E

CHELSEA

UNION
SQUARE

EAST
VILLAGE

GREENWICH
VILLAGE

SOHO

LOWER
EAST SIDE

TRIBECA

CHINA-
TOWN

FINANCIAL
DISTRICT

W 155th St
W 155th St
076
W 153rd St
Amsterdam Ave
W 152nd St
Edgecombie Ave
Bradhurst Ave
W 151st St
W 150th St
Harlem - 148th St
W 149th St
W 148th St
W 147th St
UPPER MANHATTAN
Riverside Dr
Broadway
W 145th St
W 145th St
145th St
W 144th St
Adam Clayton Powell Jr. Blvd
W 143rd St
W 144th St
W 142nd St
W 141st St
W 142nd St
W 140th St
St Nicholas Ave
W 139th St
W 138th St
W 137th St
W 138th St
Henry Hudson Parkway
Amsterdam Ave
Blvd
137th St - City College
Broadway
W 135th St
135th St
135th St
Frederick Douglass Blvd
W 133rd St
135th St
075
W 131st St
Malcolm X
W 130th St
W 130th St
W 129th St
W 129th St
W 130th St
W 128th St
W 128th St
W 128th St
W 125th St
W 127th St
W 127th St
W 127th St
125th St
W 125th St
W 126th St
Hudson River
125th St
W 125th St
125th St
HARLEM
W 124th St
125th St
Riverside Dr
Claremont Ave
Broadway
W 123rd St
W 122nd St
Malcolm X Blvd
073
Morningside Ave
Manhattan Ave
Saint Nicholas
074
116th St - Columbia University
072
Amsterdam Ave
W 116th St
116th St
116th St
Ave
St
Eighth Ave
W 114th St
W 113th St
W 112th St
Central Park North (110th St)
NEW YORK
NEW JERSEY
Cathedral Pkwy (110th St)
W 110th St
Cathedral Pkwy (110th St)
Central Park North
W 108th St
W 106th St
Riverside Dr
W 104th St
103rd St
Central Park
W 102nd St
Amsterdam Ave
Columbus Ave
103rd St
W 100th St
West
W 98th St
97th St Transverse
Eleventh Ave
Broadway
96th St
W 97th St
W 96th St
96th St
Central Park
W 94th St
W 92nd St

D

NEW JERSEY

NEW YORK

Henry Hudson Parkway

Riverside Dr

Hudson River

Joe DiMaggio Hwy

Riverside Dr

Lincoln Tunnel

Twelfth Ave (West Side Hwy)

Eleventh Ave

Eleventh Ave

Eleventh Ave

Amsterdam Ave

Tenth Ave

Tenth Ave

Ninth Ave

Ninth Ave

Eighth Ave

Eighth Ave

Central Park West

Columbus Ave

Broadway

Broadway

Seventh Ave

7th Ave

Seventh Ave

Sixth Ave

UPPER WEST SIDE

LINCOLN SQUARE

HELL'S KITCHEN

GARMENT DISTRICT

J. Kennedy Onassis Reservoir

The Lake

Central Park

W 90th St
W 89th St
W 88th St
W 87th St
W 86th St
86th St
86th St
W 85th St
W 84th St
W 83rd St
W 82nd St
81st St - Museum of Natural History
W 81st St
W 80th St
79th St
W 78th St
071
W 77th St
W 76th St
W 75th St
W 74th St
72nd St
W 72nd St
72nd St
W 71st St
W 69th St
W 66th St
66th St - Lincoln Center
W 65th St
W 63rd St
069
070
W 61st St
59th St - Columbus Circle
W 59th St
Central Park South
067
W 57th St
060
065
W 56th St
066
059
064
7th Ave
068
W 54th St
056
W 53rd St
W 52nd St
50th St - Broadway
50th St
50th St
49th St
47-50 Sts - Rockefeller Ctr
W 48th St
053
W 47th St
W 46th St
W 45th St
42nd St - Bryant Park
W 44th St
Times Sq 42nd St
W 43rd St
051
W 42nd St
42nd St - Port Authority
W 41st St
050
W 40th St
049
Lincoln Tunnel
W 38th St
W 36th St
34th St - Penn Station
34th St - Hudson Yards
W 34th St
34th St - Penn Station
Herald Sq
040
W 33rd St
34th St - Herald Sq
038
039
Penn Station
W 31st St
Penn Station
W 30th St
28th St
036
037

E

035

026

W 23rd St

023rd
St

23rd
St

23rd
St

West

Tenth Ave

032

W 21st St

CHELSEA

W 20th St

W 19th St

18th
St

Sixth Ave

034

031

W 18th St

033

Side Hwy

W 17th St

W 16th St

6th Ave
14th St

W 15th St

030

14th
St

028

029

8th Ave
14th St

MEATPACKING
DISTRICT

Gaansevort St

Eighth Ave

W 12th St

WEST
VILLAGE

Horatio St

Waverly Pl.

Jane St

027

Bethune St

W 3rd St

West Side Hwy

Washington St

Bleecker St

W 10th St

Christopher St

Christopher
St

W 4th St -
Washington
Sq

020

Seventh Ave S

Bedford St

Hudson St

Houston
St

Clarkson St
W Houston St

Varick St

Greenwich St

NEW YORK
NEW JERSEY

Hoboken

021

022

Newark St

Canal St

Hudson River

Hoboken / NJ
Transit Terminal

Washington St

Canal St

Greenwich St

West Side Hwy

Holland Tunnel

023

Hudson River

Marin Blvd

Washington St

Jersey
City

Warren St

Columbus Dr

Wayne St

Montgomery St

York St

Sussex St

0   1 km

Manhattan: Southern Tip
World Trade Center, Financial District, Civic Center

1

005 Seven World Trade Center

001 One World Trade Center

Aerial view of the World Trade Center

1

004 World Trade Center Transportation Hub

002 National September 11 Museum

003 National September 11 Memorial

Photo: Iwan Baan

One World Trade Center (formerly known as Freedom Tower) — Obelisk

001 E

285 Fulton Street,
World Trade Center
David Childs of SOM
2013

E to World Trade Center
R W to Cortland Street
A C 1 2 3 to Chambers Street
J Z 4 5 to Fulton Street
PATH **trains** to World Trade Center,
Ferry to Brookfield Place-Battery Park

1

"The completion of One World Trade Center marks a major milestone in the history of New York City. More than 13 years in the making, the 104-story, 3.5-million-square-foot, 1,776-foot tower [a symbolic reference to the year of American independence] — the tallest in the Western Hemisphere — recaptures the New York skyline, reasserts Lower Manhattan's preeminence as a global business center, and establishes a new civic icon for the country." So says the text I was sent by the architects of this building, which for the moment is the tallest in the city. In its early planning stages, it was called the Freedom Tower and is occasionally still referred to as such. SOM's statement is by and large correct. Yet, I tend to agree with those critics who voice their disappointment in this building, as the result is quite conservative and cautiously executed. From a distance, the mighty tower surely conveys an assertive image, and seen through the city's streets from many vantage points, it may look notably bold, dynamic, and even edgy. Its simultaneously elemental and complex geometry of massive, chamfered corners and steep, interlocking triangles produces mostly uneven, octagonal floor plates. Certain aspects of the building recall the basic forms and parameters of the original Twin Towers — its square base, square roof, and the fact that its parapets mark the height of the Twins, while its stainless steel, cable-stayed spire, and LED beacon tip pierce the sky 440 feet (134 meters) higher. However, up close the building is encircled by visually intrusive security bollards, barriers, and gates; their clumsiness alarms visitors wandering in the shadow of this colossus, and they make people feel quite uneasy. Rather than glancing at the sky, our attention seems to be fixed to the ground. The building sits uncomfortably on top of its 20-story, windowless concrete base, quite foreign

to the overall obelisk-like form despite the fact that it is cloaked in a skin of elegant butterfly-shaped glass louvers. It looks and feels like a bunker. The enormous public spaces that the Twins used to house at their bases are all gone and now you can't even peek inside the new lobbies, unless you work in the tower or purchase an expensive ticket to go up to the Observatory. Now that the building is finished we can analyze it by contrasting it to the original winning design by New York-based architect Daniel Libeskind, who envisioned public gardens at his tower's top and bottom, or semifinalist proposals by architects Rafael Viñoly, Norman Foster, Greg Lynn, Steven Holl, Richard Meier, Peter Eisenman, and others. In comparison, the resulting tower is quite banal, which explains why so many people would rather see the original Twins rebuilt.

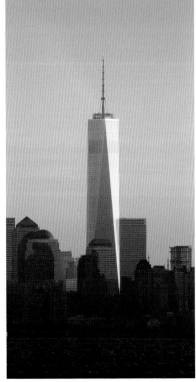

Photos: James Ewing | OTTO

National September 11 Memorial and Museum — Twin Pools

180 Greenwich Street,
World Trade Center
*Michael Arad of Handel Architects,
Peter Walker of PWP Landscape
Architecture; 2011*

002 E

🄴 to World Trade Center
🆁 🆆 to Cortland Street
🅰🅲🄵🄶🄶 to Chambers Street
🄹🅉🄸🄶 to Fulton Street
***PATH* trains** to World Trade Center,
Ferry to Brookfield Place-Battery Park

The National September 11 Memorial is a vast cobblestone plaza with moss and grass, planted with four hundred swamp white oak trees, which form a permeable canopy. It occupies half of the 16-acre (13.5-hectare) World Trade Center site in Lower Manhattan. The Memorial was designed by the Israeli-American architect Michael Arad, presently a partner at New York-based Handel Architects, in collaboration with the landscape architect Peter Walker of PWP Landscape Architecture, based in Berkeley, California. Arad won 2004 international competition to design the World Trade Center Memorial, which attracted 5,200 entries from all over the world. The winning scheme, titled *Reflecting Absence*, features two square voids, one acre each in size, placed exactly in the footprints of the Twin Towers that once stood there. The 30-foot (9-meter)-deep reflecting pools puncture the flat expanse of the plaza and form empty vessels lined by waterfalls cascading over dark gray granite walls. The Memorial Plaza is an integral part of the redeveloped World Trade Center complex, and it reaches and connects the site to the dense urban fabric of the city around it. The names of the nearly 3,000 victims, who died at the World Trade Center, as well as in Washington, D.C. and Pennsylvania on September 11, are incised into darkly patinated bronze panels lining the perimeters of both pools and appear as shadows during the day, marked by the absence of bronze. At night, the hovering wing-like profile of the panels is illuminated from within, lighting each name with a soft glow. The design, as built, is a product of many compromises achieved through years of negotiations between numerous parties, including state, local, and federal officials, the Port Authority of New York and New Jersey, the developer Larry Silverstein, the Ground Zero master planner Daniel Libeskind, the victims' families, and the state-city Lower Manhattan Development Corporation. The Memorial Foundation headed by then-mayor Michael Bloomberg replaced the LMDC in 2006. Due to many conflicts between these myriad parties, as well as the necessity to respond to the budget cuts and security concerns, Arad's original design, which had memorial galleries below ground where curtains of water would have served as backdrops for the names of the dead, and that would have encouraged the visitors to look up, was scrapped.

Photo: Jin Lee

1

**Pavilion, National
September 11 Memorial
Museum — Glacier**
180 Greenwich Street,
World Trade Center
Snøhetta
2014

003 E

E to World Trade Center
R W to Cortland Street
A C 1 2 3 to Chambers Street
J Z 4 5 to Fulton Street
PATH trains to World Trade Center,
Ferry to Brookfield Place-Battery Park

Snøhetta, which when translated means "mountain with a hood of snow," is one of the highest mountains in Norway. It is also the name of the most famous Norwegian architectural firm. Their website identifies Snøhetta as a place that nobody is from, but anyone can go to, and it is a tradition of sorts for the entire global staff of the company, which maintains a New York office, to hike the mountain together every year. Interestingly, the company's Pavilion of the National September 11 Memorial Museum also recalls a kind of small snow and ice formation, a glacier. The Pavilion is the entry point into the underground museum designed by New York architects Davis Brody Bond. With its low, horizontal form and its uplifting geometry, the structure acts as a bridge between opposing worlds — between the Memorial and the Museum, the above-ground and below-ground, the light and dark, and between collective and individual experiences. The architects employed inclined, reflective, and transparent surfaces to encourage people to walk up close, touch, and gaze into the building. Within the atrium stand two structural columns rescued from the original towers. Although removed from their former location and function, they mark the site with their own original aesthetic gesture. The alternating reflective treatment of the facade mirrors the changing seasons, revealing the Pavilion's differing qualities throughout the year.

Oculus, World Trade Center Transportation Hub — Bird

1

GATE
5F

Oculus, World Trade Center
Transportation Hub — Bird
185 Greenwich Street,
World Trade Center
Santiago Calatrava
2016

004 **E**

E to World Trade Center
R W to Cortland Street
A C 1 2 3 to Chambers Street
J Z 4 5 to Fulton Street
PATH **trains** to World Trade Center,
Ferry to Brookfield Place-Battery Park

Shopping has become our most desired experience and, inevitably, architecture revolves around it. There are now many models of shopping — in addition to traditional street and mall shopping there is also airport shopping, museum shopping, train-station shopping, and so on. The Oculus, designed by New York-based, Spanish architect Santiago Calatrava, belongs to the latter. Yet, its visitors may go shopping there all day and not even suspect that it is, in fact, a train station, because the trains are buried somewhere in the basement. And why should it matter? One of our most treasured public spaces, Grand Central Station, which was Calatrava's model for his Oculus project, isn't about its trains at all. And who would really want to hang out at Grand Central's cramped and dilapidated regional train and subway platforms anyway? It is celebrated for the dignifying grandeur of its sumptuous main concourse with celestial ceiling, spacious waiting and exhibition halls, restaurants with vaulted ceilings, and of course, a great deal of shopping. So in the end, the Oculus is also more a shopping mall than a train station. But it is primarily a great civic gesture, and many would agree that it is one of the most exhilarating spaces in the whole world. When the project was just announced in early 2004, Calatrava cited the image of a bird released from a child's hands as his inspiration. This gesture is captured in pointy, cantilevered steel rafters that spring up and inscribe two 350-foot (107-meter)-wide arches, which flank the Oculus' central axis. This whopping, column-free, elliptical space is 350 feet long and 115 feet (35 meters) across at its widest. Between two hovering wings, a 330-foot (100-meter)-high operable skylight frames a slice of New York sky; it opens on temperate days, as well as every year on September 11. Sure, these generous dimensions do not seem to quite fit within a smallish pedestrian plaza, which is more like a leftover space between the surrounding forest of office towers and the tiny entry doors at the two opposing corners. Yet, the tight space around this exotic bird of a building gets along well with New York's ever-growing density and the way structures overlap and reflect in one another, producing an incredibly rich urban collage visually and experientially.

1

Photo: Alex Fradkin

54

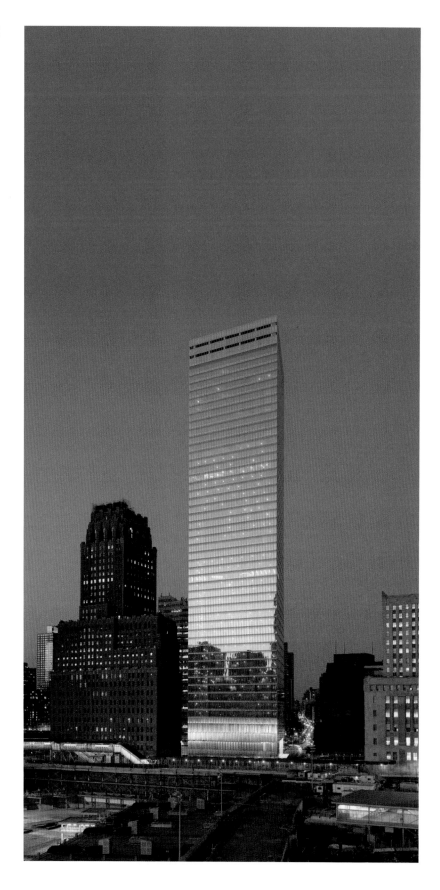

Seven World Trade Center — Diamond

250 Greenwich Street,
World Trade Center
*David Childs of SOM
and James Carpenter*; 2006

005 E

🔵 **E** to World Trade Center
R **W** to Cortland Street
🔵🔵🔵🔵🔵 to Chambers Street
🔵🔵🔵🔵🔵 to Fulton Street
***PATH* trains** to World Trade Center,
Ferry to Brookfield Place-Battery Park

One may question whether Seven World Trade Center is an icon at all. Its flat-topped, constantly elusive, and hard-to-remember image is not easy to spot in the sea of other similar towers. But the memory of the leaning and falling original 47-story Seven World Trade Center is unforgettable. It was the last building to collapse in the terrorist attacks on September 11, 2001. Built from 2002 to 2006, the new 52-story structure was the first piece of the new World Trade Center, which makes it symbolic and one of the most iconic features of early-21st-century New York. It is located immediately north of the main 16-acre (6.5-hectare) site of the World Trade Center and diagonally across Vesey Street from One World Trade Center, also designed by SOM. The new building, a pure extrusion, occupies a site that is smaller than the original, which was a trapezoidal shape. It has a diamond-shaped footprint due to the restoration of Greenwich Street. This intervention created a triangular piece of land, which is the site of the new Silverstein Family Park. New York-based landscape architect Ken Smith designed it, and the space features Jeff Koons's iconic *Balloon Flower (Red)* sculpture and a fountain. The tower sits on top of 10-story base occupied by a Con-solidated Edison substation that supplies electrical service to Lower Manhattan. The design is a collaboration between David Childs of SOM and New York-based architect-artist James Carpenter, who used ultra-clear, low-iron glass to provide reflectivity and light within the bends that are between the glazed floors to accentuate reflected sunlight. The sky-scraper's entire surface is calibrated to create the illusion of depth. It is animated with light, which evolves naturally by day with the changing exterior conditions and has programmed LED projection sequences by night. The cube-like base emanates blue light at night, while during the day it provides white light to the lobby. At dusk it transitions to violet and back to blue. Inside the main lobby, world-renowned New York artist Jenny Holzer created a large light installation with glowing text that moves across wide plastic panels. The entire 65-foot (20-meter)-wide wall changes color according to the time of day. The artist worked with the developer's wife, Klara Silverstein, to select poetry for this art installation. In my interview with Carpenter in March 2007, he stressed the following: "Quality, transmission, and reflection of light can be fully and totally controlled. We can achieve virtually any level of filtration of play of light by combining glass, coatings, and various additives between layers of glass. Our task is to pick or invent appropriate types and combinations of glass to achieve any desirable effect."

1

Fulton Center — Fedora

1

Fulton Center — Fedora

200 Broadway,
Financial District
*Grimshaw Architects
and James Carpenter*
2014

Ⓡ Ⓦ to Cortland Street
Ⓐ Ⓒ Ⓙ Ⓩ ② ③ ④ ⑤ to Fulton Street

Ask anyone who ever visited New York and it is very likely that their experience with its mass transit system here was, to put it mildly, dismaying. Yes, it is more densely laid out than any other metro system, operates around the clock, is quick and amazingly efficient when running well, but it can be a horror show when it is not working properly. It is also memorable for its attention-grabbing musicians and acrobats, who provide world-class entertainment as a bonus for a Metrocard swipe. But seriously, how could the experience of getting from one neighborhood to another in such a global city such as ours be more disgraceful? American architectural historian Vincent Scully had a point when he contrasted the current Penn Station with the original one by

saying, "One entered the city like a god. One scuttles in now like a rat." Knowing all this, an encounter with the Fulton Center, the point of conversion for eleven subway lines, and where 300,000 commuters cross paths daily, is shocking in a good way. The station is a fantastic celebration of generous space, ambient light, and pulsating urbanity; the sky is folded deep into its underground space, animated with the most delicate and constantly changing light patterns. The Center is one of the most dignifying public places in the city. As it is situated just one block away from the Oculus, one sure hopes that these two new civic places are a glimpse of how our subway system, train, bus, and ferry terminals, and airports may look like in the future. The Center sits in a glass pavilion that keeps the neighborhood's landmarks in view, so it is easy for people to orient themselves upon their arrival. With a clear boundary between indoors and outdoors, it feels like an enclosed park, which draws office workers who bring food here during their lunch hours. How wonderful to see New Yorkers slow down for once to appreciate beautiful space and light! The transit hub's atrium rises

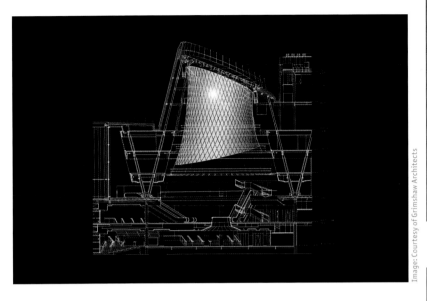

Image: Courtesy of Grimshaw Architects

1

to 112 feet (34 meters) and is topped by a conical dome centered on the concourse below. From above this structure does not look like any other building in the city and may recall a fedora dropped in a hurry by a mysterious giant. The central architectural concept of redirecting natural light deep into the transit environment culminates in the design of the dome's interior and a new integrated artwork titled *Sky Reflector-Net,* designed by architect-artist James Carpenter. It is made of almost one thousand diamond-shaped, aluminum panels that redirect light and intensify the reflection of the sky above. Held in place by hundreds of tensioned cables and high-strength rods and thousands of stainless-steel components, the reflector is so large that it feels like the whole station sits inside of it.

Photo: James Ewing

New Amsterdam Pavilion — Propeller

Peter Minuit Plaza on
State Street, Financial District
*Ben van Berkel and
Caroline Bos of UNStudio
with Handel Architects*
2009

1 to South Ferry
4 5 to Bawling Green
R W to Whitehall Street
Staten Island Ferry to Whitehall Terminal

Commissioned by the Battery Conservancy, the New Amsterdam Pavilion by Amsterdam-based architects Ben van Berkel and Caroline Bos of UNStudio, was presented as a gift from the Dutch government to the people of New York. It marks the 400th anniversary of Henry Hudson's quest for a Northwest Passage to Asia, which led to his 1609 landing in New York Harbor on behalf of the Dutch East India Company. The four-blade, propeller-like pavilion is an info kiosk, and a dynamic art, light, and media installation. It shares the story of its location with visitors and discusses the four-century relationship between the Netherlands and New York, which was originally founded as New Amsterdam in 1624. Reaching a height of just 10 feet 6 inches (3.2 meters) and occupying a mere 400 square feet (37 square meters), the size of the tiniest New York studio apartments, the Pavilion projects an energy and fluidity rarely seen in architectural projects. The structure is a steel frame and clad in polyurethane-coated plywood. It is a sleek, seemingly twisting object that succeeds in drawing attention to its hyperactive form. After midnight it is accentuated by multicolored neon lighting, making it look like an exotic flower.

Photos: James D'Addio

Photo: Courtesy of SHoP Architects

Pier 15 — Watermark
78 South Street,
Financial District
SHoP Architects
2011

008 E

Ⓐ Ⓒ Ⓙ Ⓩ ➋ ➌ ➍ ➎
to Fulton Street, Wall Street
Ferry to Pier 11

1

A pier is not a building. We can't walk around it to confront it frontally or walk into it through a front door. It is more like a playground with both outdoor and indoor spaces, a roof platform to enjoy the sun, the breeze, and very cool views of the city and its immense harbor. This, of course, does not make it less of a piece of architecture, especially since the architects of so many of the most successful contemporary buildings are quickly moving away from the design of stark, free-standing objects, and instead are focusing on creating engaging environments that blend in seamlessly with whatever surrounds them. Pier 15, located in the heart of the Financial District, is plugged into the East River Waterfront Esplanade, a two-mile (three-kilometer)-long public promenade that has become a constellation of intimately-scaled recreational and commercial spaces along the water's edge. The new pier is a two-story pleasure structure. Tacked into the ground floor is a ship-dock and ticketing office for the popular Hornblower Cruises & Events, cafés, and a maritime education forum. The roof serves as a second-level deck, that despite its low elevation allows spectacular, far-reaching views. Vistas like these have become one of the most profitable commodities in New York; however, they are offered free of charge here. The pier is situated very close to the must-see Brooklyn Bridge. Modern, cozy, and well-integrated seating, handrails, and lighting feature original, well-crafted details in pleasing-to-the-eye concrete, steel, aluminum, glass, and wood. Several grassy lawns on the top level complete this sleek park, which seemingly floats over the harbor like an attractive watermark.

Photo: Magda Biernat

New York by Gehry (originally known as Beekman Tower) — Gehry
8 Spruce Street, Civic Center
near Brooklyn Bridge
and City Hall
Frank Gehry
2011

009 E

Ⓐ Ⓒ Ⓙ Ⓩ ② ③ ④ ⑤ to Fulton Street
⑥ to Brooklyn Bridge

After his 2001 retrospective exhibition, *Frank Gehry: Architect* at New York's Guggenheim, the completion of his IAC Building near the High Line in 2007, and several other interiors in the city, Gehry, a Canadian-born American who resides in Los Angeles and is the most famous of all living architects, finally realized a major high-rise in a city of high-rises. Marketed as "New York by Gehry," his first skyscraper is not as ambitious as two of the architect's earlier attempts to bring his signature style architecture to the city — the 40-story "cloudlike" Guggenheim Museum that was intended to rise from the East River near the South Street Seaport (2000), and the Atlantic Yards development (2006) in Brooklyn, which proceeded without him. The 76-story mixed-use tower, just south of City Hall and Brooklyn Bridge, succeeds as a good companion to such nearby skyscrapers as Cass Gilbert's 1912 Woolworth Building, and McKim, Mead & White's 1914 Municipal Building. And it produces a completely unique vertical statement that is unlike any other building in the city or anywhere else in the world. In contrast to most contemporary buildings on such a scale, the Gehry tower attracts interest at any distance. Growing out of a conventional five-story base faced in reddish-tan brick, the shiny tower is masterfully clad in stainless steel, and appears as a mesmerizing object both from the Brooklyn waterfront and up close. Its rumpled skin evokes numerous metaphors — from delicate fabric to stormy sea water. It looks endlessly fascinating and keeps the eye constantly intrigued. Walking around this freestanding multifaceted structure reveals that its south side is as flat as a blade; it is hidden from most views and typically avoided by photographers. But this abrupt change of geometry gives the building a particular edginess. The tower's base, the least interesting part of the project, houses a public school, a garage, and all the amenities expected for luxury living. There are over 900 rental apartments. While the tower's exterior is almost entirely wrapped in undulating facades, all of the interiors are rectilinear. Still, the fluid form of the tower enables every unit to be distinguished by a slightly different configuration. At the edges, a system of overlapping

Photo: Vladimir Paperny

bay windows creates unique conditions, in which residents may find themselves literally suspended over the city. The project represented a new digital design approach by the architect who pioneered the use of CATIA, digital 3D-modeling software that enabled architects and builders to dream up and realize ever more visually arresting structures. Nicolai Ouroussoff, who was then the *New York Times* architecture critic, wrote, "8 Spruce Street seems to crystallize a particular moment in cultural history, in this case the turning point from the modern to the digital age."

Manhattan: Lower Manhattan
Bowery, Lower East Side, East Village, NoHo

2

010 Sperone Westwater Gallery

011 New Museum of Contemporary Art

Sperone Westwater Gallery — 010 E
Elevator
257 Bowery, Bowery
Foster + Partners
with Adamson Associates
2010

🄵🄼 to 2 Avenue
🄱🄳 to Grand Street

Sperone Westwater Gallery, designed by London-based architect Norman Foster, and situated on the Bowery just one block away from the New Museum, is among a cluster of innovative projects built here in recent years. The area, known for its kitchen-equipment shops, and which is still dotted with these rough-looking stores, is being transformed into a vibrant artistic hub. The new building is a response to a desire to rethink the way in which the viewer traditionally engages with art in the context of a gallery. The narrow site measures 25 feet by 100 feet (7.6 meters by 30.5 meters), typical of lots in the Bowery. The result is a building whose verticality is naturally emphasized. Its focal point is a 12-foot by

20-foot (3.6-meter by 6-meter) room, which can move vertically, like an elevator. It is both a physical response to the gallery's dynamic program and a kinetic addition to the street. The gallery/elevator can either function as a regular elevator or be positioned to extend any one of the four upper-floor galleries, whereupon an additional elevator and stairs in the back provide alternative routes up through the building. Its bright red exterior is visible through the translucent, milled-glass facade; the gentle pace at which it travels contrasts nicely with the chaotic activity of the city and traffic outside. The gallery/elevator's exposed concrete shaft and mechanics draw on an aesthetic and scale appropriate to the building's neighborhood context, which, albeit in transition, remains largely industrial. To me, one of the most fascinating details about this small project is Foster's devotion to resolving every detail, which is exposed in one of his sketches. On it, Foster wrote to his project architect in New York, "Michael, I've been worrying about appearance of the entrance canopy... Feel free to call me."

Photo: Nigel Young/Foster + Partners

New Museum of Contemporary Art — Stack

011 E

235 Bowery Street, Bowery
*Kazuyo Sejima and Ryue
Nishizawa of SANAA with Gensler*
2007

🄵 🄼 to 2 Avenue
🄱 🄳 to Grand Street

Architecture is just like art or poetry — one masterpiece may lead to another, but there is no guarantee. The New Museum of Contemporary Art, the only New York City building designed by the Tokyo-based architects Kazuyo Sejima and Ryue Nishizawa, whose partnership's name is SANAA, is not among their best works. It is a pity because, based on my many interviews with leading international architects, I can testify that among its peers SANAA is a most admired and revered practice. SANAA's buildings are typically celebrated for their poetic forms, lightness, restraint, and beautifully conceived and executed details. Unfortunately, here their dramatic stack of seven shifted rectangular boxes of various sizes and heights does not quite succeed. Perhaps this has to do with the quality of construction that the architects may not have been able to achieve here. Nevertheless, the form is perfectly iconic. It works not only as a memorable new logotype for the museum, but the building's platforms are also ingeniously used by curators to display some large artworks. The building's geometry raises many questions. It is so striking and convincing outside — the entire building, including most of its windows, is clad in a seamless, anodized expanded aluminum mesh — but these moves are barely noticeable on the inside. Apart from a few smallish windows and skylights, the galleries are sealed off from each other, from the building's promising form, and from the vibrant neighborhood around. The most rewarding space is on the ground floor, where a nearly 15-foot (4.5-meter)-tall plane of clear glass along the Bowery, stretches across the full width of the site. It includes the public entrance, bookstore, and café on one side of the elevator core and the loading dock on the other, where back-of-house activities and the movement of artworks are in full view of passersby. Throughout this space, which is largely open to the public without a ticket, nothing is hidden. That includes the building's structure and guts — the ducts, the sprinklers, and even the fireproofing material. What is intriguing now is whether SANAA's original form will retain its iconic look; that will depend on what Rem Koolhaas, the famous Dutch architect who was recently selected for the Museum's expansion, will do next. It is not an easy building to add to.

Photo: Dean Kaufman

215 Chrystie Street —
Fish Scales
215 Chrystie Street, Bowery
*Jacques Herzog and Pierre
de Meuron of Herzog & de Meuron
with Beyer Blinder Belle*
2017

012 E

🇫 to 2 Avenue
🅱 🅳 Ⓜ to Broadway-Lafayette Street

Located in the Bowery, the rapidly evolving cultural and artistic district in the center of Lower Manhattan, 215 Chrystie Street is a mixed-use building, with the trendy Public Hotel surrounded by a lush garden at the base, and 11 condominiums on top. The hotel features restaurants, a rooftop bar, and Public Arts, a popular event and party venue. In their description of 215 Chrystie Street, Jacques Herzog and Pierre de Meuron, Basel-based architects, pointed out that the framework for the site and the building's form had already been established before they were even invited to work on the project. This restricts us mainly to discussing the building's skin, and it is exactly what distinguishes this building from all others. The architects pushed the structure to the exterior envelop, where it follows the grid of the large floor-to-ceiling window bays. This introduces a depth to the facades, where slabs and columns are directly expressed as raw concrete, and liberates the interiors from freestanding columns. To introduce a sense of scale and to further foster the expression of each individual floor, each column is slightly inclined. Note the building's unusually sculptural, full-height corner that functions as a visual anchor for the entire structure. It is made up of "braided" columns alternating their inclines from floor to floor. Each hotel room has one large window that sits between the columns and slabs. The windows are framed with polished aluminum and are tilted outwards from ceiling to floor to create more space for the room, and to increase the reflection of the sky in the glass. The resulting pattern recalls fish scales. This profile was also meant to improve privacy, but little did the architects know that the gently tilted, full-height glass would embolden hotel guests to perform all kinds of acts naked, pressed against the glass, which entertains onlookers on the street and irritates neighbors all around. Taking advantage of the fact that structural forces decrease at the top of the building, every second column, including at the corners, is omitted in the apartment tower above the hotel. This strategy maximizes square footage as well as the views and transparency on all residential floors.

Photos: Alex Fradkin

Switch Building — Switch
109 Norfolk Street,
Lower East Side
Mimi Hoang and Eric Bunge
of nArchitects
2006

013 E

F J M Z to Delancey Street-Essex Street

This petite seven-story apartment building with its characteristic Galvalume (aluminum-zinc-alloy coated sheet steel) panel facade features an art gallery at the bottom, four floor-through apartments in the middle, and a duplex penthouse.

The building's design reflects nArchitects' "switching" concept. To coax some variety from the facades and create different floor plans, the architects alternate the layout of the angled bay windows at the front and deep balconies at the back on every other floor. The double-height spaces between balconies and bay windows maximize sunlight and views. This results in an unusually dynamic and memorable image. Note that the building is situated right next to the Blue Tower by Bernard Tschumi and near other recently built and under-construction experimental buildings in this part of the Lower East Side.

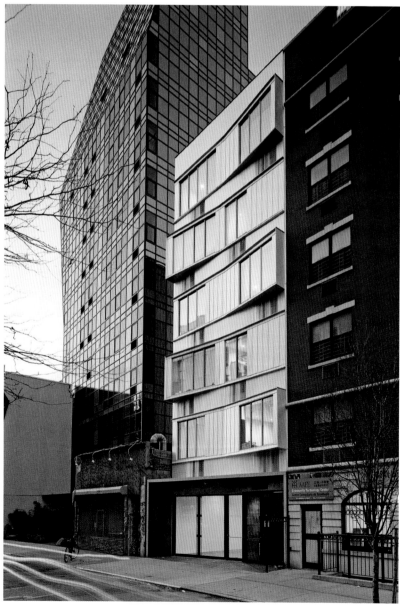

Photo: Courtesy of nARCHITECTS

Blue Tower — Blue
105 Norfolk Street,
Lower East Side
Bernard Tschumi
with SLCE Architects
2007

F J M Z to Delancey Street-Essex Street

Named after the color of its pixelated, glass facade, this striking 17-story building is only the second structure Swiss-born, New York and Paris-based architect, Bernard Tschumi has realized in New York (his first, Alfred Lerner Hall at Columbia University, was built in 1999). The fact that this accomplished architect, based in New York since mid-1970s and who served as Dean of Columbia University's Architecture School from 1988 to 2003, built so little in his home town says a lot about the challenges of realizing truly innovative architecture in the city. Despite the Blue Tower's signature envelope, unlike Tschumi's first building, it can hardly be called innovative. Even in the architect's own description of the project he cites the constraints of the New York City zoning code as the main driver for his architectural statement. For one of the key Deconstructivists of his generation, this is hardly worthy reasoning. In that context, the building is surely a missed opportunity. Still, note how the south side of the tower bulges as it goes up, looming over the commercial property next-door. Also, examine some of the corners that feature up to four angled walls. Unlike conventional curtain wall construction, the system employed unitized components that were glazed, sealed, assembled in the factory, shipped to the site, and then hoisted into place. The curtain wall system is composed of clear-glass pieces, vision-glass pieces tinted blue, and opaque spandrel panels in four shades of blue to better reflect the diverse character of the Lower East Side, and blend with the sky.

Photo: Peter Mauss

40 Bond Street — Grid

015 E

40 Bond Street, NoHo
*Jacques Herzog
and Pierre de Meuron
of Herzog & de Meuron
with Handel Architects*
2007

Ⓑ Ⓓ Ⓕ Ⓜ to Broadway-Lafayette Street
❻ to Bleecker Street
Ⓡ Ⓦ to 8 Street-NYU

Occupying five narrow lots, the cleanly-detailed, glass-clad building at 40 Bond Street is embedded into richly decorated fabric of brownstones, red-brick, and cast-iron lofts, contrasting strongly with this historical part of NoHo with its cobblestone streets. Designed by Jacques Herzog and Pierre de Meuron, working with Handel Architects, this 10-story residential building stacks two distinct typologies for living — the townhouse with five duplexes and the apartment block above with half of the upper floors set back from the street to allow for terraces, while the top level is reserved for a full-floor penthouse. The five townhouses reintroduce the scale of the original lots. Each townhouse has a recessed entry porch across its street frontage and a garden to the rear. The porches are separated from the street by a cast-aluminum gate, its fluid design inspired by street graffiti. The entrance lobby for the condominiums is a narrow, double-height slash that divides the aluminum screen between three townhouses on one side and two on the other, and connects the street with a communal garden at the back. The facade's design is a spare reinvention of the cast-iron building that is typical of both NoHo and SoHo. The structure of the building is pushed to the exterior and follows the grid of the large floor-to-ceiling window bays. Slabs and columns are clad with gently curved glass covers. They wrap over the entire facade, which visually dissolves into a play of translucency, light, and reflection.

Photo: Iwan Baan

The Standard, East Village (formerly Cooper Square Hotel) — Shark's Fin

016 E

25 Cooper Square, East Village
Carlos Zapata
2008

Ⓑ Ⓓ Ⓕ Ⓜ to Broadway-Lafayette Street
❻ to Astor Place
Ⓡ Ⓦ to 8 Street-NYU

Violently wedged mid-block, facing Cooper Square and situated among unremarkable historical tenement buildings, the 21-story The Standard, East Village hotel looks utterly out of place in this largely still low-rise East Village neighborhood. Wrapped in fritted glass, the tower is unequivocally iconic. Yet, its undefined, even somewhat outrageous form provoked a range of nicknames — from the "shark's fin," suggesting its aggressiveness and sheer size, however sleek, to "splinter" and "iceberg" for its fractured form and

Photo: Courtesy of Carlos Zapata Studio

milky white glazed skin. Another blunt tag applied to this edifice by its neighbors is "Dubai," which says something about the building's unrooted and foreign character.

51 Astor Place — Origami

51 Astor Place, East Village
*Fumihiko Maki of Maki
and Associates with
Adamson Associates Architects*
2013

6 to Astor Place
R W to 8 Street-NYU

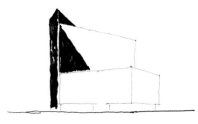

Glass versus stone seems to be a genuine concern to quite a few people as more and more glass buildings find their way to neighborhoods that were until recently dominated by prewar stone facades. 51 Astor Place is a strong building that, despite its amiable and handsomely proportioned form, addresses the issue of context head on. As one of the few buildings in the city that occupies its own block, it is not surprising that it positions itself toward the surrounding architecture with an attitude. Yet, it does so with decency and respect. Composed of three sharply angled cascading prisms — from 13 floors along the Fourth Avenue to four floors on Third Avenue — the building is designed by Tokyo-based architect, Fumihiko Maki who is also the architect of 72-story Four World Trade Center.

Despite being a strong contrast to older buildings in Astor Place and the kind of architecture that we associate with the East Village, this origami-like building is hardly the first that tries to move this neighborhood into the future. Gwathmey Siegel & Associates Architects' 21-story glass tower, which is shaped in plan like an amoeba, as well as Thom Mayne's 41 Cooper Square, and Carlos Zapata's The Standard, East Village hotel, all sharply contrast with the neighborhood, so 51 Astor Place can hardly be considered as a game-changer in this regard. More so, the building's striking, dark-tinted mirrored facade appears to be quite sensitive and even timeless. 51 Astor Place replaced Cooper Union's School of Engineering Building; its design was chosen in a limited architectural competition. The complex, stepped volume varies in appearance from different vantage points. Note the lovely painted aluminum sculpture by Keith Haring at the triangular corner of the Third Avenue and 8th Street, and more surprisingly, Jeff Koons's glitzy *Balloon Rabbit (Red)* sculpture that occupies pretty much the entire lobby along the Fourth Avenue. In my 2018 interview with Maki, at his Tokyo studio, the architect said, "Today, we have so many strange buildings. So many architects try to achieve something that was never seen before. My approach is minimal. I try to avoid making unnecessarily complex forms and textures. It is a kind of discipline that I impose on myself. Design is somewhat unconscious. There is always something unknown in the process." He also explained that he would not use concrete (his favorite material) outside of Japan because "for sure, the project would be killed," referring to the difficulty of controlling delicate quality of construction.

Photo and drawing: Courtesy of Maki and Associates

Cooper Union Academic Building — Armor

2

Cooper Union Academic
Building — Armor
41 Cooper Square, East Village
*Thom Mayne of Morphosis
with Gruzen Samton Architects*
2009

018 E

6 to Astor Place
R **W** to 8 Street-NYU

As a Cooper Union graduate who spent most of my freshman year at the two-story, 1912 Hewitt Building that was replaced by this new academic building designed by Los Angeles and New York-based architect Thom Mayne, I followed its construction quite attentively. It was excruciating to watch, particularly towards completion, because even a few weeks before the opening there was absolutely nothing to see but the building's unattractive mass getting bigger and bigger. Finally, its precariously folded, creased, and cracked armor, made up of thin stainless-steel perforated panels (which reportedly accounted for one-third of the building's total cost), came into place right over the glazed envelope. It was amazing to witness how an ugly duckling of a building was transformed day-by-day into a beautiful edifice. Not surprisingly, not everyone likes the result; many see the building as unfinished and even disturbing. In fact, this structure is so controversial that upon completion it was cited both as the most beautiful and the ugliest building in New York, depending on whom was asked. "I am aware of how little people are affected by architecture, though they seem to be paying attention to some of my projects, such as the Cooper Union building here in New York," Thom Mayne told me in a 2016 interview. "Perhaps because it has a certain amount of eccentricity in it that attracts people. I am interested in multiple forces, in the unfinished, the misalignments of various elements. Neutrality is something that has no quality. To produce something neutral is a failure. Everything is in constant flux. We are constantly rethinking what architecture is. I have been interested in an architecture of complexity — an architecture promoting difference, the pursuit of ambiguity, the coexistence of apparent contradictions." According to the architect, the new academic building was a response to the school's goal of creating an iconic structure. Moreover, the building is infinitely more interesting than its image. It needs to be walked around to examine its beautiful dress, which also provides shading control, and going inside is a must. However, such a visit needs to be arranged with the school, as the guard will not let you go past his desk. Internally, the building is

Photo: Alex Fradkin

Drawing by Thom Mayne

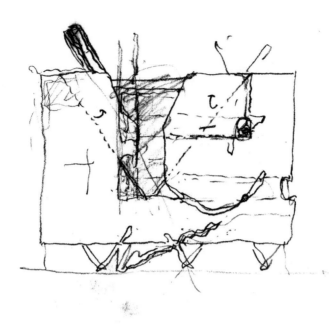

2

conceived as a vehicle to foster collaboration and cross-disciplinary dialog among the college's three schools, previously housed in separate buildings. Rome's famous Spanish Steps must have served as a true inspiration for this beautifully arranged space, as a 20-foot (6-meter)-wide grand, yet informal stair ascending four stories forms the new building's social armature by connecting the ground-floor lobby and a glazed double-high student lounge overlooking the city. An undulating all-white metal lattice envelops it. Angled and folded skybridges crisscross the nine-floor-high atrium. An exhibition gallery, visible from the lobby and a 200-seat auditorium with mesh-sculpted ceiling are located one level below grade.

Photo: Iwan Baan

Manhattan: Downtown

Greenwich Village, West Village, SoHo, TriBeCa

3

025 The Stealth Building

3

The New School University Center —
Dig Dug Facade

3

SCHOOL
RSITY CENTER

The New School University Center — Dig Dug Facade

019 E

63 5th Avenue, Greenwich Village
Skidmore, Owings & Merrill (SOM)
2013

F M to 14 Street
L N Q R W 4 5 6
to 14 Street-Union Square

Located at the corner of 14th Street and Fifth Avenue, the New School's University Center, is a 16-story campus, squashed into a single building with a seven-story base and nine-story residential tower. It distinguishes itself with striking dented glazed stairs that diagonally traverse the lower floors and recall the Dig Dug computer game. The facades are meticulously embellished in a variety of rectangular and triangular hand-finished brass shingles that tilt in and out generating a busy and slightly dizzying pattern, except where they have been sliced away to expose the stairs. Note the razor-sharp canopies over the ground floor, particularly right at the corner. Such bold and aggressive geometry is usually reserved for spires. Broad perimeter "communicating stairs" allow navigation between floors at a more leisurely pace, while linking many of the building's social spots, which are dubbed "sky quads." The Center's compact layout purposely mixes learning, living, dining, and socializing spaces to promote interdisciplinary learning and cultivate discussion and debate. It also houses design studios, laboratories, classrooms, art studios, a gym, the main university library, a large auditorium, cafés, and numerous flexible academic and social spaces.

Photo: James Ewing

173–176 Perry Street
Condominium and 165
Charles Street — Trio
173–176 Perry Street,
165 Charles Street, West Village
Richard Meier
2002, 2005

① to Christopher Street-Sheridan Square
Ⓐ Ⓒ Ⓔ Ⓛ to 14 Street
PATH trains to Christopher Street Station

Richard Meier's own website categorizes these three slender buildings, lined up along West Street and overlooking the Hudson River, as "icons." They certainly are iconic and that is not only due to their characteristic towering presence. They also were the architect's first projects built from the ground up in New York City, after he had practiced here for three decades. And, according to Meier's website, none of the architect's subsequent works done in New York made it into the site's own "iconic" category. Despite the fact that all three buildings vary in size and were built for two different developers, they are perceived as a single project. Two of the 15-story towers have different footprints and were built three years earlier. Meier was not responsible for their interiors. However, he was hired by several individual owners to design their apartments. The original two buildings feature one apartment per floor. The third 16-story tower on the south side was entirely designed by Meier. Except for four apartments with double height living rooms on the second floor and a single

penthouse, there are two apartments per floor. All three buildings are clad in insulating laminated glass and white metal panels with shadowboxes at the curtain wall expressing the individual floor plates. The buildings are particularly fascinating at night, as their interiors are put on display for those voyeurs who are not indifferent to the glamorous lifestyles of the rich and famous people who call these buildings home. In our interview in 2005, Meier explained to me: "We are going to provide curtains, designed by us. So, people can do whatever they want once the curtains are pulled." As it turned out, and to the full satisfaction of the architect, many residents want to do "whatever" with their blinds way up.

3

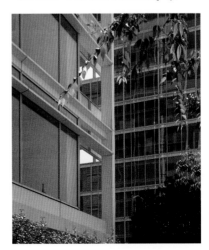

Spring Street Salt Shed — Crown

336 Spring Street, SoHo
WXY, Dattner Architects
2015

021 E

A C E 1 to Canal Street

How can something as banal as a salt shed rise to the level of architecture, let alone be iconic? We know from Nikolaus Pevsner, a German-British architectural historian that, "A bicycle shed is a building," while "Lincoln Cathedral is a piece of architecture." So it is particularly satisfactory to see that in fact, sheds can be shaped into architecture, and therefore this project is exemplary. Located on the trapezoidal block bound by West, Canal, and Spring Streets, the Salt Shed is a freestanding part of a new large sanitation garage to the north, screened with a diaphanous facade. The Shed's polygonal form is inspired by salt crystals, but due to its outward tapering, continuous outer wall it looks more like a faceted crown, especially when dramatically lit from the bottom at night. Rising nearly 70 feet (21 meters), the windowless folded structure is built of cast-in-place, 6-foot (1.8-meter)-thick concrete walls. The result is so beautiful that it attracts photographers, who use it as a background for photo shoots. The building's only function is to serve as a storage container for 5,000 tons of de-icing salt piled 40 feet (12 meters) high for the roads of Lower Manhattan. Though its purpose is mundane, this sculptural building may be Manhattan's most artistic piece of architecture.

3

Photo: Dattner Architects/Albert Vecerka/Esto

497 Greenwich Building — Wave

497 Greenwich, SoHo

Winka Dubbeldam of Archi-Tectonics with David Hotson Architect

2004

`022` `E`

Ⓐ Ⓒ Ⓔ ❶ to Canal Street

A building is more than its facade, but sometimes it is a facade that makes a building — and it is not for nothing that Cesar Pelli once remarked, "Sometimes architecture is just a matter of a quarter of an inch." These thoughts are so true of 497 Greenwich, a residential building located on the edge of SoHo and designed by Dutch-American New York-based architect Winka Dubbeldam, as its architecture is precisely found within its facade in just a quarter of an inch. It is put together from glass panels; each precisely customized and manufactured in Barcelona and Hong Kong, and then assembled in Brooklyn. The resulting facade of intricately folded glass panels constitutes a continuously-fluid glass wave, which is seemingly seamless due to the use of completely transparent seams. This facade not only goes up the height of the 11-story building but doubles in width by covering four additional floors on top of the adjacent renovated six-story brick building, a former warehouse. At the time of this building's completion the late Herbert Muschamp, then the *New York Times* architecture critic, wrote: "Dubbeldam's folds are philosophically as well as visually grounded... [She] crystallizes urban complexity within the discrete architectural object." In 2005, Dubbeldam, who lives in the building, told me, "We used the facade of the building as a kind of connective membrane or interface to the city. We literally took the zoning code and inflected two code systems into it — the straight and the incline. By doing that, we created a more integrated whole of folded planes, which pushed some apartments out over the street, suspending inhabitants, and other apartments were pulled away so it seems that the sky collapses onto them. The Internet brought public space right into our living room, so there is no longer a real separation between private and public; I wanted to investigate and celebrate this. There is a strange, almost voyeuristic link between the neighbors, as there are moments where one looks straight down or up through other apartments."

Photo and drawing: Courtesy of Archi-Tectonics

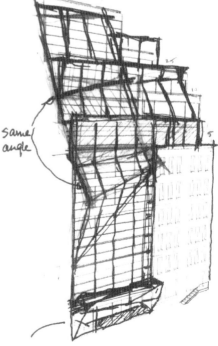

Unhistorical Townhouse —
Gaudí
187 Franklin Street, TriBeCa
Jeremy Edmiston
of System Architects
2018

❶ to Franklin Street
Ⓐ Ⓒ Ⓔ to Canal Street

Antonio Gaudí, the late 19th- and early 20th-century Spanish architect, frequently worked with brick and wrought iron grilles, and this is the obvious association when one stumbles upon this single-family townhouse designed by the New York-based Australian-American architect Jeremy Edmiston. His flamboyantly undulating brick facade with its wildly curved and angled windows is visually reinforced with steel, mesh-like balconies. While there is no doubt that the Catalonian genius would have brought this facade's characteristic flame-like stacks of red brick all the way down to the pavement, here in TriBeCa the original ground floor had to be preserved. The complex, parametric geometry of the facade is mirrored in the domestic spaces inside, where an interior wall of twisted brick anchors the back of the house,

its curves providing seating, shelving, and a fireplace. The radical twists and folds of the facade are all accomplished with standard-sized bricks, the material characteristic of the historic neighborhood where most buildings were built as warehouses. The Landmarks Preservation Commission approved the bold design in a rare unanimous vote. In our 2017 interview, Edmiston said: "This project is a response to a domestic life of a family in a city. How do you program that? Their lives are lived on both sides of that wall. The entire building is just one room deep, which means that every room is on the backside of that facade. Every activity in their domestic lives is written into it." And when I pressed the architect for his reason to employ curves here, he responded bluntly, "The universe is warped. Isn't architecture a part of it?"

3

Photos: Courtesy of System Architects

Photo: Alex Fradkin

56 Leonard Street —
Jenga Tower
56 Leonard Street, TriBeCa
*Jacques Herzog and Pierre
de Meuron of Herzog & de Meuron*
2016

024 E

1 to Franklin Street
J N Q R W Z 6 to Canal Street

According to Jacques Herzog and Pierre de Meuron, the architects of 56 Leonard Street, this project was conceived as "houses stacked in the sky" to address the sameness and anonymity of the ubiquitous generic residential high-rises that we are all familiar with. The Basel-based architects, who now maintain a busy New York office, resolved their 57-story tower as a stack of apartments; the building is now by far the tallest in TriBeCa. Individual apartments progressively pull apart like pixels, and as the structure rises, the depths of the cantilevers of apartment corners, terraces, balconies, and large bay windows increase proportionally, earning the building its nickname — the Jenga Tower. The key selling point of this luxury condominium is that each "house" is unique and identifiable within the overall stack. Reportedly, only five out of 145 apartments are repeated, and no two floor plates are the same. Originally, the tower's design was even more dramatically pixelated, but value engineering following the 2008 global financial crisis made it more conventional. At the tower's base, superstar British artist Anish Kapoor designed a bulbous mirrored sculpture, which at the time of writing was not in place. Curiously, the sculptor owns a large apartment close to the tower's pixelated top, so there is a chance that the phantom sculpture will eventually assume its intended place.

3

Photo: V. Belogolovsky

The Stealth Building —
Stealth
93 Reade Street, TriBeCa
Dan Wood and Amale Andraos
of WORKac
2016

Ⓐ Ⓒ Ⓙ Ⓩ ❶ ❷ ❸ to Chambers Street
Ⓡ Ⓦ to City Hall
❹ ❺ ❻ to Brooklyn Bridge-City Hall

Just as you would expect from the Stealth Building, its most remarkable element is a sharply-folded roof addition that is invisible from the street and can only be spotted from taller buildings around it or with the help of Google Earth. The roof addition over this historical building in TriBeCa had to be invisible per the requirements of the New York City Landmarks Commission. This residential development of four condominiums consists of a complete gut-renovation, and a new construction behind one of New York's most beautiful commercial cast-iron facades, which was manufactured in 1857. To make sure that the resulting roof addition would be completely invisible from the street level, its form was achieved by tracing the cone of vision from the farthest point on the ground, from which the building's rounded pediment and roof parapets can be seen. The sculptural addition serves as the top floor of the triplex penthouse that occupies the fifth, sixth, and seventh floors. A secluded terrace is sunken behind the pediment, while the old elevator bulkhead is

repurposed as a hot-tub room. On the facade, 25 new Corinthian column capitals
adorned with foliage motifs stand in for
long-lost originals. The new capitals were
cast not in iron, but in malleable glass-
fiber-reinforced concrete based on a CNC-
cut foam model. In 2015, I interviewed
the Stealth Building's architects, Rhode
Island-born Dan Wood and Beirut-born
Amale Andraos, the couple that founded
New York-based office of WORKac. In that
conversation, Wood said: "Our goal is to
unseal buildings and apply urban strategies to architecture. We are concerned
with opening up buildings as an extension
of the idea of opening up ourselves to nature and to reinventing building systems.
We work to engage peoples' curiosity and
creativity and try to make them think

about their relationship with the environment in a different way, to begin to question how we live, and realize how complex
this relationship is, especially in cities."

3

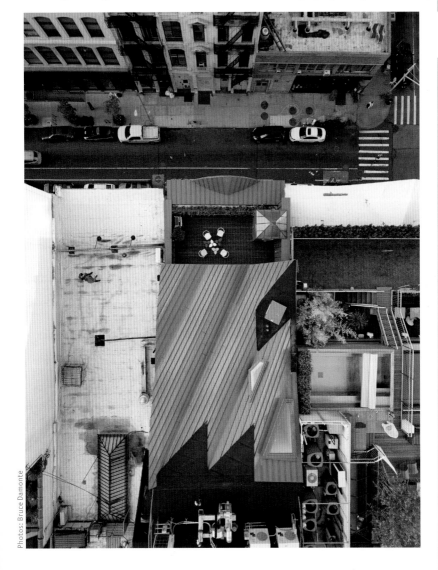

Manhattan: West Side
Meatpacking District, Chelsea, Hudson Yards

4

035 HL23

026 High Line Park

4

High Line Park — Trestle

Photo: Courtesy of Diller Scofidio + Renfro/Iwan Baan

High Line Park — Trestle

026 E

10th Avenue, Chelsea,
from Gansevoort Street
to 34th Street

*Diller Scofidio + Renfro, James Corner Field
Operations, garden design by Piet Oudolf*
Phase I, 2009; Phase II, 2011;
Phase III, 2014

Ⓐ Ⓒ Ⓔ Ⓛ to 14 Street
Ⓒ Ⓔ to 23 Street
❼ to 34 Street-Hudson Yards

If you haven't been here, you can't quite imagine what a contemporary urban park can be. This 1.5-mile (2.3-kilometer)-long public park was built on an abandoned elevated railroad trestle that was put up in 1934 to replace the street-level railroad tracks along 10th Avenue where trains frequently killed pedestrians (which is why it was dubbed "Death Avenue.") Originally, the elevated railroad ran from 34th Street to St. John's Park Terminal at Spring Street. It was designed to go through the center of blocks rather than over 10th Avenue to connect directly to factories and warehouses, thus allowing milk, meat, produce, and raw material and manufactured goods to be loaded and unloaded inside buildings without disturbing street traffic. By 1960, the southernmost section of the line was demolished due to disuse and in 1980 the remaining part saw its last train. After that the trestle stood unused and fell into disrepair; it was slated

for demolition in the 1990s. In 1999, local residents Joshua David and Robert Hammond formed the nonprofit Friends of the High Line. They advocated for the line's preservation and reuse as public open space, so that it would become an elevated greenway, similar to the Promenade Plantée in Paris. Fundraising was organized by fashion designer Diane von Fürstenberg, her husband, the businessman Barry Diller (both of their headquarters were built next to the High Line), and city government. They succeeded in attracting enough funds to organize an international design competition and to build the park. The new High Line stretches from Gansevoort Street in the Meatpacking District, where the new Whitney Museum is built, through Chelsea, to the Hudson Rail Yards, now the biggest construction site in the city. Numerous new buildings were recently added next to the High Line, as a direct result of its redevelopment. When I asked New York-based architect Steven Holl about his dream project back in 2005, his response was the following: "Well, my real dream project is the High Line. I've been working on the possibilities for what I think is an incredibly important piece of New York City for the last 20 years. One day it will become an elevated green strip that moves through the city. It will be a public space that gives you a different point of view. Not just elevated point of view, but also sound and

silence. You can't really hear the city from there. It is so quiet and wonderful." The park was also discussed in my 2009 interview with British-born landscape architect James Corner, the founder of New York-based James Corner Field Operations whose contribution to the High Line original design is often overlooked. Here is his view: "Ultimately, the High Line was about creating an elevated landscape that people could stroll along and experience the city. But it was important that this landscape capture the same unusual, magical, strange qualities of the original post-industrial High Line landscape — a structure marked by melancholy, emergent plant growth, detachment and a certain unruliness. The paving system is designed in such a way that concrete, rail tracks, stone ballast, and planting all intermix, or bleed into one another, much like the original meadow that grew upon the old rail bed." Finally, here is a quote from my 2016 interview with Liz Diller, Polish-born founding partner of famed New York-based practice Diller Scofidio + Renfro: "Look at the High Line project — formulated around the idea to create a space for doing nothing! It is so foreign for New York, even exotic. You can't do anything there — you can't throw a ball, ride a bicycle, bring your dog... But is the High Line model's viral success due in large part to the fact that we questioned the convention of traditional public space?"

Whitney Museum of American Art — Battleship

4

Whitney Museum of American Art — Battleship
99 Gansevoort Street,
Meatpacking District
Renzo Piano Building Workshop
with Cooper Robertson
2015

027 E

A C E L to 14 Street

It is important to say something not only about the building that was built in the heart of the reinvented Meatpacking District but also what kind of building it could have been. Occupying one of the most desirable spots in New York, between the southern tip of the High Line at Gansevoort Street and Hudson River Greenway promenade, separated by West Street highway, the project had all the right ingredients to make something absolutely marvelous here. It had the right site, fantastic client with a generous budget, and most importantly, we had the right architect, one of the best in the world, Genoa and Paris-based Renzo Piano who maintains a New York office to oversee a number of his projects here and elsewhere in the U.S. But somehow the resulting building does not break the kind of new ground that the Centre Pompidou did when Piano designed it with British architect Richard Rogers back in 1971. And if groundbreaking design was not the Whitney's goal then why would they ask Piano to design this project in the first place? The new Whitney is a strange eight-story jumble of industrial parts that are straight, angled, inverted, piled up, and jut out. It is clad in pale blue-gray steel panels, some blank, others punched with glass openings and louvers. Look the other way and you will forget the building almost immediately; it is too strange and too busy. Yet, if rearranged, these nautical-looking forms may be imagined as a battleship. It has firmly docked with broad open-air decks facing the city, not the Hudson; that decision turned the building and its outdoor steel stairs at the upper floors into a fantastic viewing platform. These stairs distract visitors from both indoor and outdoor art viewing that may be quite intense at times, and help to dissolve a building that lacks Piano's signature beautiful detailing, into its surroundings, New York from vantage points that you have never seen before. And that, one may argue, is the whole point of any art. Still, I wonder if the Whitney considers architecture to be an art form on its own or do they try to curtail any clash between architecture and art?

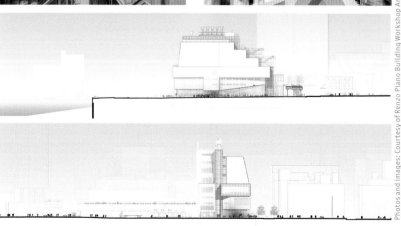

Photo: Iwan Baan

**The Standard, High Line
(formerly The Standard) —
Crutch**
848 Washington Street,
Meatpacking District
*Ennead Architects
(formerly Polshek Partnership)*
2009

028 E

Ⓐ Ⓒ Ⓔ Ⓛ to 14 Street

This 18-story luxury boutique hotel hovers high above the southern end of the High Line Park and the Meatpacking District, an area largely occupied by two-story 19th and 20th century manufacturing lofts and industrial buildings that are now filled with restaurants, high-end boutiques, and art galleries. The hotel, which Ennead Architects' website describes as "iconic," is shaped like two hinged slabs of concrete and glass. It is raised 57 feet (17 meters) above street level on several massive sculptural piers. On the east side of the structure a single, slightly inclined concrete pier, which recalls a crutch, provides most of the support for half of the tower and allows open fire-escape stairs to hang from it. These expressive concrete piers evoke some of the Brutalist structures by Le Corbusier who, of course, contributed his ideas to the design of the United Nations Building on the East Side of Midtown. The most original aspect about the building is its relationship to the city grid and to the High Line that shoots right between its

legs at the height of 30 feet (9 meters). Then, of course, there is a lot of glass, and as with some of the other buildings in the city, it seems to encourage exhibitionistic tendencies in its occupants. Provocative posing in front of the massive floor-to-ceiling windows never fails to draw the attention of pedestrians, wandering around in great numbers here, and of course, the press. The following is the official statement from the hotel's management published by the *New York Post*: "When we built The Standard, we hoped it would provide the best views of New York looking out. We didn't anticipate that it would also provide those views looking in."

Photo: V. Belogolovsky

4

837 Washington — Twist

837 Washington Street,
Meatpacking District
Morris Adjmi of MA
2014

029 E

Ⓐ Ⓒ Ⓔ Ⓛ to 14 Street

837 Washington Street is a new commercial office building in the Meatpacking District, where the rigid 1811 Manhattan street grid collides with the older, picturesque streets of Greenwich Village. Designed by New Orleans native and New York-based architect Morris Adjmi of MA, the building comprises two distinct but coexisting elements: a new twisting steel-and-glass volume and a

rehabilitated 1938 Art Deco brick warehouse. The warehouse retains much of its no-frills character, including a restored, cantilevered metal canopy and an ad hoc arrangement of garage doors, which have been repurposed as oversized storefront windows. The new volume's twisted floor plates, inspired by the collision of the city's street grids, are clad in a curtain wall designed to complement the original building's factory-style fenestration, while its bold structural steel exoskeleton evokes the High Line across the street. The design also incorporates beds of native plants that fill the voids created by the twisted floors, further echoing the High Line's post-industrial garden setting, while softening the interior spaces and reducing stormwater runoff.

4

The Porter House — Hunchback `030` `E`
66 Ninth Avenue, Chelsea
SHoP Architects
2003

A **C** **E** **L** to 14 Street

Located in the West Village, The Porter House is a renovation and conversion of a six-story warehouse, built in 1905, into residential condominiums. Added to the structure is a new six-story addition that rises from the existing fifth floor, bringing the overall structure to the total of 10 stories. The 8-foot (2.5-meter) cantilever of the new addition along the building's southern side contributes to the building's characteristic profile evoking a hunchback posture. The new addition is accentuated by a custom-fabricated zinc panel system for the facade and floor-to-ceiling windows, as well as the verticality of the structure and the unique interface between the exteriors of the original Renaissance Revival facade. To minimize material waste, the project team worked closely with the fabricator, and used sheet-metal industry software to develop an elevation pattern based on the most efficient layout of panels from standard sheets of material. Since the panels were cut and bent directly from SHoP's digital files, an economy of scale was achieved in the manufacturing process. The resulting facades feature windows and zinc panels of different widths that appear to be highly customized. In our 2013 interview at SHoP's Manhattan office, architect Gregg Pasquarelli, the founding partner of the practice, said: "We never limit ourselves to simply designing an image. Part of our initial concept is always about knowing how something is going to be built. For us, an idea is not a shape. That's not how we start. We start by saying — let's use copper or let's use glass. Well, how big does the glass come? What are the ways it gets attached? What is the easiest way to put it on the building? Into how many pieces can I break it? How sharp of an angle can I make before it becomes expensive? All that thinking starts on day one. So, the building emerges out of the logic, of how it works, and how it is put together. How does that logic work on the inside? How does that logic work within the urban context? How does everything work with the technology that is needed to put everything together? That's how we always worked. It is great to show a very complex form to a client and hear them say: "You can't build that!" And to be able to say to them: "Yes, actually we can — and here is how you do it."

Chelsea Modern — Zigzag

 031 E

447 West 18th Street, Chelsea
Audrey Matlock Architect
2009

C E L to 23 Street

Photo: Audrey Matlock

This 12-story residential building designed by New York architect Audrey Matlock is all about its wavy facade. All of its apartments feature floor-to-ceiling glass with built-in window blinds. The building's facade is conceived as a series of multistory blue glass bands. Their zigzagging horizontally from end to end is a direct response to the building's dynamic location at the Chelsea contemporary art district near the High Line and the Hudson River. The ground-floor duplex units are reserved for artists and collectors; each one has street access and a private rear garden. All of the upper units have terraces overlooking the inner garden. Both inner and roof gardens are shared by all residents.

Metal Shutter House — Barley-Break Game

 032 E

524 West 19th Street, Chelsea
Shigeru Ban with Dean Maltz
2011

4

A C E L to 14 Street

Photo: Michael Moran

It is true that most memorable buildings in New York are distinguished by their facades; as is the 11-story Metal Shutter House in Chelsea designed by Tokyo-based architect Shigeru Ban. Yet, this building's identity is not something permanent, as it is with most other structures. The building's appearance depends on the mood of its tenants; each of the nine apartments has full control over its exterior presentation. All the apartments extend through the entire depth of the building, with front and back exposures that can be completely concealed or revealed with the help of operable perforated metal screens, from which the Shutter House takes its name. Moreover, on a good day, the entire glass wall at both ends of each condo can be pivoted up, transforming a whole apartment into an open outdoor space with double-height, 20-foot (6-meter)-high living rooms. This flexibility ensures that the building's facades will never look the same, while their "moving" voids and solids evoke a Barley-Break game. The shutters echo typical after-hours shutters used by galleries and stores in the area, as well as at the building's own ground-floor gallery-retail space. In our 2003 interview, Ban told me: "The most important thing about architecture for me is people's reactions. I am happy when I can meet the people who will move into my houses. That is why I don't like working on apartment complexes, since I don't know who is going to live there. Occasionally, I like visiting my museums or churches, and hiding behind one of the paper columns [Ban's name has become synonymous in architecture with cardboard tubes employed in many of his projects, though he decided to avoid it in this high-end project] simply to observe the visitors. I enjoy doing that a lot."

The IAC Building — Sail
555 West 18th Street, Chelsea
Frank Gehry
2007

033 E

🅐 🅒 🅔 🅛 to 14 Street

It is partly due to the IAC Building, the first project Frank Gehry built in New York, that driving along the West Side Highway has become such a sightseeing pleasure — the slower the better! Located between 18th and 19th Streets and directly facing the highway, this nine-story building is one of the most beautiful new, iconic additions to Manhattan's West Side. Highly visible from the High Line (at least until Bjarke Ingel's two twisted condo towers, called the XI, are built), which hovers just 150 feet (45 meters) to the east, the IAC's expressively sculpted glass facades evoke a boat with white sails gliding along the Hudson. What a nice contrast with Midtown's hard-edged corporate towers. The IAC Building serves as world headquarters for New York businessman Barry Diller's media and Internet empire. An avid yachtsman, whose super-yacht is often docked across the highway at Chelsea Piers, Diller himself suggested a sail boat as a design motif. He also insisted on the building's color — white, and glass for the material. The lobby, stretching the building's entire length, is conceived as a public living room for the neighborhood and special events. Its back wall is dominated by a 118-foot (36-meter)-long video wall, where projected video art and abstract color compositions are visible from the street. The building's facades may not seem nearly as contorted as some of Gehry's other creations. Still, to achieve the right subtlety and desired visual effects was quite a challenge. The so-called glass sails were put together out of large flat panels, each one bent through a process carried out on-site, known as cold-warping. The glass facade of the concrete structure is insulated and has a special coating and patterned ceramic particles, small white enamel dots that are silk-screened onto the glass below waist-height, and above head-height to improve energy efficiency, while leaving an eye-level band of clear glass to allow expansive river views from within.

Photo: Alex Fradkin

Photo: Roland Halbe

100 Eleventh Avenue — Kaleidoscope

034 E

100 Eleventh Avenue, Chelsea
Jean Nouvel with Beyer Blinder Belle Architects
2010

A C E L to 14 Street

Paris-based architect Jean Nouvel designed this 23-story residential tower with a rounded corner at the intersection of 19th Street and the West Side Highway. The building is locked between two contrasting facades that respond to two different contexts — a pixelated glass curtain wall, overlooking the Hudson River and Gehry's bulging glass IAC Building facade across the street, and a black brick wall volume punched with windows of various sizes, facing the High Line and the city. On the lower seven stories, the building's front is surrounded by a freestanding scaffold-like curtain wall, placed 15 feet (4.5 meters) away from the glass. Behind this structure is a semi-enclosed atrium that features fully-grown trees that seem to float in midair. The most prominent feature here is the glass facade. It was designed from within and described by the architect as "a vision machine," referring to the kaleidoscopic views offered by the windows. They were inspired by the compound eye of an insect. The glass curtain wall consists of large, floor-height panels, each the size of a room. The panels are further fragmented into smaller windows of various sizes that tilt at different angles, resulting in different levels of transparency throughout the facade. Different glass coatings add another layer of depth as the light plays across the facade. When seen from the West Side Highway or the Hudson, the building's pixelated facade evokes Impressionist paintings by Claude Monet; particularly the *Houses of Parliament* series, with their dreamy reflections in the Thames depicting different times of the day and weather conditions.

HL23 — Cyborg

517 West 23rd Street, Chelsea
*Neil Denari Architects
with Marc Rosenbaum
Architects*
2012

035 E

C E 1 to 23 Street

HL23 is a reflection of the fascinating, sci-fi, futuristic world of Los Angeles-based architect Neil Denari, a fan of British high-tech and everything digital. His only New York building is a kind of embodiment of a cyborg, a creature of both organic and biomechatronic body parts; it stands out and fits right in at the same time. Moreover, its presence right next to the High Line could not be more perfect. This fact is engraved in its coded name — HL23, the High Line at its intersection with 23rd Street. The slim-fit, beautifully crafted, condominium building starts with the street-level, two-story art gallery and continues its 14-story ascent with one unit per floor, each exposed to three distinct yet coherent facades. It splits, bends and cantilevers,

curves, and transitions from structure to graphics, and from 3D stainless-steel panels to glass. The building's geometry is driven by the restrictions of the zoning envelope and by the architect's interest in achieving complexity through simple tectonic operations. In our 2011 interview, Denari said: "Our work is not about communicating anything or telling stories like books, but I believe it has a capacity to collapse and blur two, three dimensions of information into one. The collapse and merging of different technologies describes the evolution of my work — away from fixed codes toward new formal possibilities, complexities, and fluidity in architecture. I am interested in compressing many of the various dimensions of the surrounding world. The new digital technologies help us to loosen the Cartesian world and push in the direction of free and more expressionistic form. We are trying to do spaces and forms that are noticeable and interactive. I am interested in more subtle and smoother geometry. The work is very abstract and it doesn't recall anything in particular. It is an ongoing project."

4

Hotel Americano — Paranja 036 D
518 West 27th Street, Chelsea
Enrique Norten of Ten Arquitectos
2011

C E 1 to 23 Street

Located on West 27th Street, between 10th and 11th Avenues next to the High Line, the Hotel Americano, designed by New York-based Mexican architect Enrique Norten, sits on what is one of New York's most active gallery streets by day and vibrant club scenes by night. The facade of the hotel directly reflects this dichotomy. The hotel floors are set back from the street behind a stainless-steel mesh screen that reflects sunlight beautifully throughout the day, and creates a much needed buffer between the street-side hotel rooms and the all-night activity of the bars and clubs below. The screen, the most prominent paranja-like feature of the building's facade, offers unusually softened city views, while providing privacy to the hotel's guests. The building houses a ground-floor restaurant facing a garden in the back, and a roof deck with a pool, bar, and garden terrace. Its height alleviates the surrounding concrete jungle with reflective surfaces, water, greenery, views over the High Line, and New York's ever-changing cityscape. During my 2015

Photo: Courtesy of Ten Arquitectos

interview with Norten, the architect told me: "I want architecture to shift focus from its preoccupation with form and object making to public space making. Personally, I am more and more interested in the experience than in the object. In the beginning, I was more interested in the object. But what is more important to the people who visit a city — to take with them that iconic form that they will never forget or the unique experience? I like the kind of architecture that underlines and enhances our experience."

520 West 28th Street — Zaha 037 D
520 West 28th Street, Chelsea
Zaha Hadid
2017

C E to 23 Street

From the very beginning 520 West 28th Street was marketed as a work of art from the genius of the Iraqi-British, London-based architect Zaha Hadid (1950–2016). Even the overhead protection system that was put up during construction was built as an art installation called *Allonge*. The boutique condominium, located just south of Hudson Yards, is by no means representative of the best of the late architect's work. Still, her iconic curves are all here, and her energy and passion for inventing a new kind of geometry makes this modestly scaled development quite special.

Photo: Hufton+Crow

In 2006, a major retrospective was held at the New York Guggenheim, to celebrated 30th anniversary of Hadid's practice. By then the Pritzker Prize winner had solidified her status as an architect who built, rather than an architect who painted, because suddenly dozens of her fantastic projects were under construction all over the world. Yet, 520 West 28th Street is the only ground-up building commission she realized in New York; to honor this I suggest calling this 11-story condominium simply "Zaha." I should, of course, mention here that Hadid lost the competition to design the High Line to Diller Scofidio + Renfro. However, 520 was not a direct commission: Hadid won a competition, beating such stars as Norman Foster, who, of course, had plenty of other chances to build in New York. What is unusual here is that 520 comes so close to the High Line that it can almost be touched by pedestrians who stroll by at its fourth-floor level and can't avoid peeking into fluidly designed apartments below, above, and directly in front. What exhibitionism — window-watching has become a common and most pleasant thing to do on the High Line! The composition of the building's elegant hand-rubbed metal facade is driven by continuous parallel lines, that loop their way skywards. These dynamic curves create distinctive aeronautical chevron patterns that mediate between the staggered floors. As the chevrons weave their way up from the ground, their folds create a multilevel design that links residence exteriors and interiors together in one sweeping movement. In my 2008 interview with Hadid, she noted about her firm's methodology, "One of the tasks I set for myself was the continuation of the unfinished project of Modernism, in the experimental spirit of the early Avant-gardes — radicalizing some of its compositional techniques like fragmentation, and layering to achieve both complexity and fluidity. We are always interested in expanding our repertoire and doing different things in different contexts, but there are some principles that we always adhere to. And one of them is to attempt to embed an object into context with a whole series of articulate relationships — trying to draw out features from the context so that in the end there is a sense of 'embeddedness,' and 'fit-ness' into the context."

4

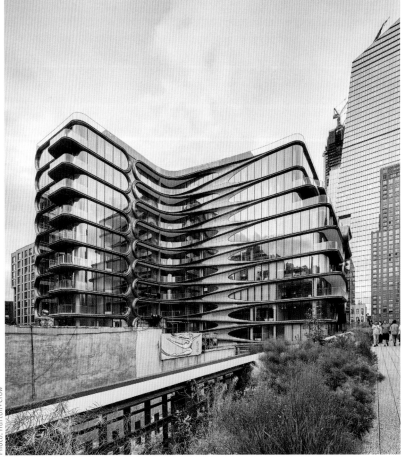

The Shed — Turtle Shell
15 Hudson Yards, Chelsea
Diller Scofidio + Renfro,
David Rockwell
2019

038 D

7 to 34 Street-Hudson Yards
A C E and *LIRR* to 34 Street-Penn St.

One could say about many of the buildings that are featured in this book, "There is nothing like it in the whole world." This is particularly relevant to the Shed, New York's new center for artistic invention, which initially was just a speculative idea. In our 2016 interview, Liz Diller of Diller Scofidio + Renfro, said, "I would urge all architects to be more active in taking part in program-making by proposing new types of projects. The Shed was initially our imaginary project that we collaborated on with David Rockwell. We proposed to the city this new type of art institution with no collection, no history, and no restraints, as far as scale or discipline. There is nothing like it in New York. It took years before there was a site and even a client. It came literally out of a dream." The Shed is designed in the spirit of such otherworldly inventions such as the "Fun Palace" proposed in 1964 for London by British architect Cedric Price, or the Centre Pompidou by Renzo Piano and Richard Rogers, realized in 1977 in Paris. The Shed is now taking shape on the far West Side, where the High Line turns towards the Hudson River at Hudson Yards, along West 30th Street between 10th and 11th Avenues. Its flexible design will accommodate the broadest range of the performance

and visual arts, and multi-disciplinary work. There are two principal components: an eight-level fixed-base building for cultural programming and support spaces, and a telescoping outer shell that looks like a turtle shell, deployed on demand over an adjoining plaza to double the building's footprint. The base building includes two expansive levels of gallery space, a versatile theater, rehearsal space, an artists' lab, and a sky-lit event space. The shell forms a vast hall that accommodates large-scale performances, installations, and events. When deployed, the shell creates a 17,200-square-foot (1,600-square-meter) light, sound, and temperature-controlled, column-free multipurpose hall with a 120-foot (37-meter) tall ceiling, that can serve an infinite variety of uses. The hall can accommodate an audience of 1,200 seated or 2,700 standing. Flexible overflow space in the two adjoining galleries in the base building allows for an expanded audience in the hall of up to 3,000. The shell, comprised of an exposed-steel diagrid frame is clad in lightweight and translucent fritted ETFE (ethylene tetrafluoroethylene, a fluorine-based plastic) cushions that are more energy efficient and less costly than glass. The shell's ceiling operates as an occupiable theatrical deck with rigging and stage lighting with high structural capacity throughout. When the shell is nested over the base building, the 19,500-square-foot (1,800-square-meter) plaza will be open public space. The building is able to expand and contract by rolling the telescoping shell on rails by means of gantry crane technology;

it takes just five minutes to completely extend the shell. The Shed's "plug and play" capability allows it to be responsive to variability in scale, media, technology, and the evolving needs of artists. "What art will look like in the future

is an open question," says Diller. The Shed is immediately adjacent to 15 Hudson Yards, an 88-story, Diller Scofidio + Renfro-designed residential tower whose plan transitions from a square at the base to a clover leaf shape at its peak.

Vessel — Pine Cone 039 D
Hudson Yards, Chelsea
Thomas Heatherwick
2019

7 to 34 Street-Hudson Yards
A C E and *LIRR* to 34 Street-Penn St.

Even though I am writing this text after the Vessel has topped out and is being readied for a 2019 opening, I still can't believe that this otherworldly project is on its way to becoming a reality. Some have called this massive art project, created by London-based designer Thomas Heatherwick, an exclamation point for Hudson Yards. It came into being thanks to the project's single client, Stephen Ross, chairman and majority owner of The Related Companies. Related is a global real-estate development firm and the developer of Hudson Yards. Ross's grand plan is to turn what was until recently the 28-acre (11-hectare) West Side Rail Yard into a mixed-use real-estate development distinguished by 16 new skyscrapers of office, residential, retail, and cultural space, as well as a new park. He envisions this entirely-from-scratch part of the city, just one subway stop from Times Square, as New York's new center. According to Ross, "The most important place in New York during Christmas time is Rockefeller Center." That was his logic for creating something even more spectacular for throughout the year, and around the clock. He said, "I wanted to have a 12-month Christmas tree." Heatherwick's Vessel is exactly that. Ross took a long road to finding an artist capable of creating such an iconic work. Initially, he had turned to five artists. They were Anish Kapoor, Jaume Plensa, Jeff Koons, Maya Lin, and Richard Serra, all famous for large-scale pieces meant to grab attention at public plazas. After investing significant resources into this process, he abandoned

Image: Forbes Massie

4

them all when a colleague at Related suggested he try Heatherwick. The designer had created the cauldron used for the Olympic flame during the 2012 Summer Olympics in London, the U.K.'s Pavilion at the Shanghai Expo 2010, and the popular Spun chair. Inspired by the ancient stepwells of India and evoking a famous *Relativity* print by the Dutch artist M.C. Escher, the Heatherwick piece is composed of 154 flights of stairs, almost 2,500 steps, and 80 connecting landing platforms. At 151 feet (46 meters) high, the structure that evokes a giant pine cone both by its form and color is made up of a steel framework and clad in polished copper-colored panels. It will be able to hold 1,000 people at a time and withstand stronger wind forces than Hurricane Sandy. Heatherwick's main goal for the piece is to raise people significantly above ground level so they can see the city — and one another — in a new way. Unfortunately, the Vessel's 15-stories will not be high enough to see beyond its own block, as it is going to be completely surrounded by much taller buildings.

Vessel — Pine Cone

4

30 Hudson Yards — Woodpecker

30 Hudson Yards, Chelsea
*Bill Pedersen of
Kohn Pedersen Fox*
2019

7 to 34 Street-Hudson Yards
A C E and *LIRR* to 34 Street-Penn St.

When complete, the 90-story 30 Hudson Yards will, at the height of 1,296 feet (395 meters), stand as the tallest tower at Hudson Yards. Located at the southeast corner of the development on West 33rd Street and 10th Avenue, the building's main lobby is accessed directly from the High Line which here, turns towards the Hudson. The tower is a part of a mixed-use complex that is comprised of another 52-story tower completed in 2016 and a retail podium, all designed by Bill Pedersen of Kohn Pedersen Fox (KPF). The two towers tilt away from the podium in opposite directions. 30 Hudson Yards will be home to the highest outdoor observation deck in the city. This platform's deeply projected, beak-like profile, suspended more than 1,000 feet in the air, contributes to the building's distinctive woodpecker-like profile. More than half of the building's space is reserved for 5,000 employees of Time Warner, a global media and entertainment company, which is expected to move here from its current home at the Time Warner Center on Columbus Circle.

4

Manhattan: Midtown South

Midtown South, Midtown, Murray Hill

5

042 Shake Shack

043 Madison Square Park Tower

041 One Madison

5

One Madison — Vertebra
23 East 22nd Street, near
Madison Square Park,
Midtown South
CetraRuddy Architecture
2013

041 E

🅑 🅓 🅡 🆆 🌀 to 23 Street

One Madison raises two critical urban design issues in New York, both having to do with height. Ever since a forest of office towers rushed to the sky in such areas as Wall Street and around Rockefeller Center, the hierarchy of what is iconic and significant was completely turned on its head. New Yorkers are long accustomed to the fact that historically and culturally important monuments such as the domes and spires of Trinity Church, St. Patrick's Cathedral, or St. Bartholomew's Church on Park Avenue, are among the shortest and visually less prominent structures in their neighborhoods. The second issue has to do with some new high-rises' extreme slenderness or height-to-width ratio. Despite One Madison's having been assigned a 22nd Street address, its presence on 23rd Street is much more prominent. It is across the street from Madison Square Park and looks directly onto Madison Avenue. The tower could be dismissed as both out of scale and out of place were it not for its strikingly elegant beauty. Still, it aggressively challenges the iconic Metropolitan Life Insurance Company Tower, which was modeled after the Campanile in Venice. It was world's tallest building for four years until the Woolworth Building was built in 1913. The two buildings are so tall and close that even though the Campanile's spire is about 80 feet (25 meters) higher it is hard to tell from the street level, which one is taller. That brings a bit of confusion to the part of New York where a particular scale and order seemed to be long established. The tower's sculptural, yet elemental form appears to be a transitional design between two other projects in the city. On the one hand, the stack of seven glass cubes of various heights that resembles a segment of vertebra, presents a lesser version of 80 South Street, a never-realized scheme designed by

Santiago Calatrava that featured twelve four-story glass cubes branched out off a slender central concrete core. On the other hand, One Madison is a more pronounced version of the Rafael Viñoly-designed 432 Park Avenue tower, which is more than twice as tall and also designed as a series of stacked multistory sections. The 50-story One Madison, reaching the height of 618 feet (188 meters), with a 12:1 slenderness ratio, sits on a base that contains five floors of services, commercial spaces, and amenities. The tower above, with floor-to-ceiling windows all around, is partially cantilevered over an existing three-story building to the east. A trophy, four-story penthouse with a terrace wrapped around on three sides and 360-degree views tops the building.

Photo: CetraRuddy Architecture, Alan Schindler

Shake Shack — Shack
Madison Square Park,
Midtown South
James Wines of SITE
2004

Drawing by James Wines

Ⓑ Ⓓ Ⓡ Ⓦ ➅ to 23 Street

The Shake Shack is a small food kiosk that can be spotted in the southern part of Madison Square Park. It was designed by New York-based architect and artist James Wines, the founder of SITE, a pioneering green architecture and environmental arts studio. The long lines in front of this modern-day "roadside" burger stand are vivid proof that it serves up delicious fare. And, it is the original location of what is now a popular international restaurant chain. The kiosk's form and design respond to the triangular shape of Daniel Burnham's Flatiron Building from 1902, which stands diagonally across 23rd Street, and are enlivened by the park's profusion of vegetation and festive atmosphere during all seasons. To provide a feeling of lightness, the service counters and kitchen areas are completely enclosed by glass. This feature makes the top sections of the structure appear to float, opening up views of surrounding trees that can be seen through the building. The graphics, designed by Paula Scher of Pentagram, refer to typical 1950s roadside hamburger stalls and convey the idea of blending the menu with the building. A large perforated metal screen filled in with English ivy covers an inclined roof and the horizontal surfaces of the canopy. In our 2016 interview, James Wines told me: "A great deal of SITE's work is about inversion, fusion, intervention, exaggeration — often just taking something apart and examining the elements of construction from a different point of view. This element of "in process," or more specifically engaging process *as* the content, has always been more interesting to me than a finished building. The point is to attack!" You may ask, attack what? "Architecture, of course!" Wines quipped.

5

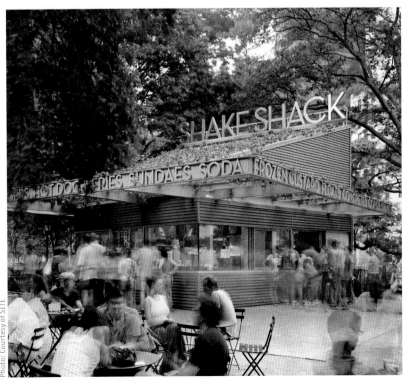

Photo: Courtesy of SITE

Madison Square Park Tower — 043 E
Thermometer
45 East 22nd Street,
Midtown South
Kohn Pedersen Fox
2018

🄵 Ⓜ Ⓡ 🅆 ❻ to 23 Street

It is hard to assess the size of this quirky tower due to its sleek glass form and barely noticeable floor divisions. Kohn Pedersen Fox designed the 64-story building to a height of 777 feet (237 meters). It is temporarily the tallest structure in the Flatiron District. (262 Fifth Avenue, designed by the Russian architecture firm Meganom, has a projected height of 1,001 feet [305 meters], and is expected to top out in the next couple of years.) Madison Square Park Tower is entirely clad in vision and spandrel-glass panels. It appropriately features floor-to-ceiling panoramic windows, since the primary selling point for this stand-alone residential condominium is its 360-degree city views. The glass tower that rises out of its four-story stone-clad base cantilevers over the next-door low-rise building. The base's material complements the mostly stone prewar buildings in this neighborhood, while the glass tower rises to a wider, slightly too-heavy pinnacle that gives the overall form a likeliness of a thermometer.

Photos: Michael Moran

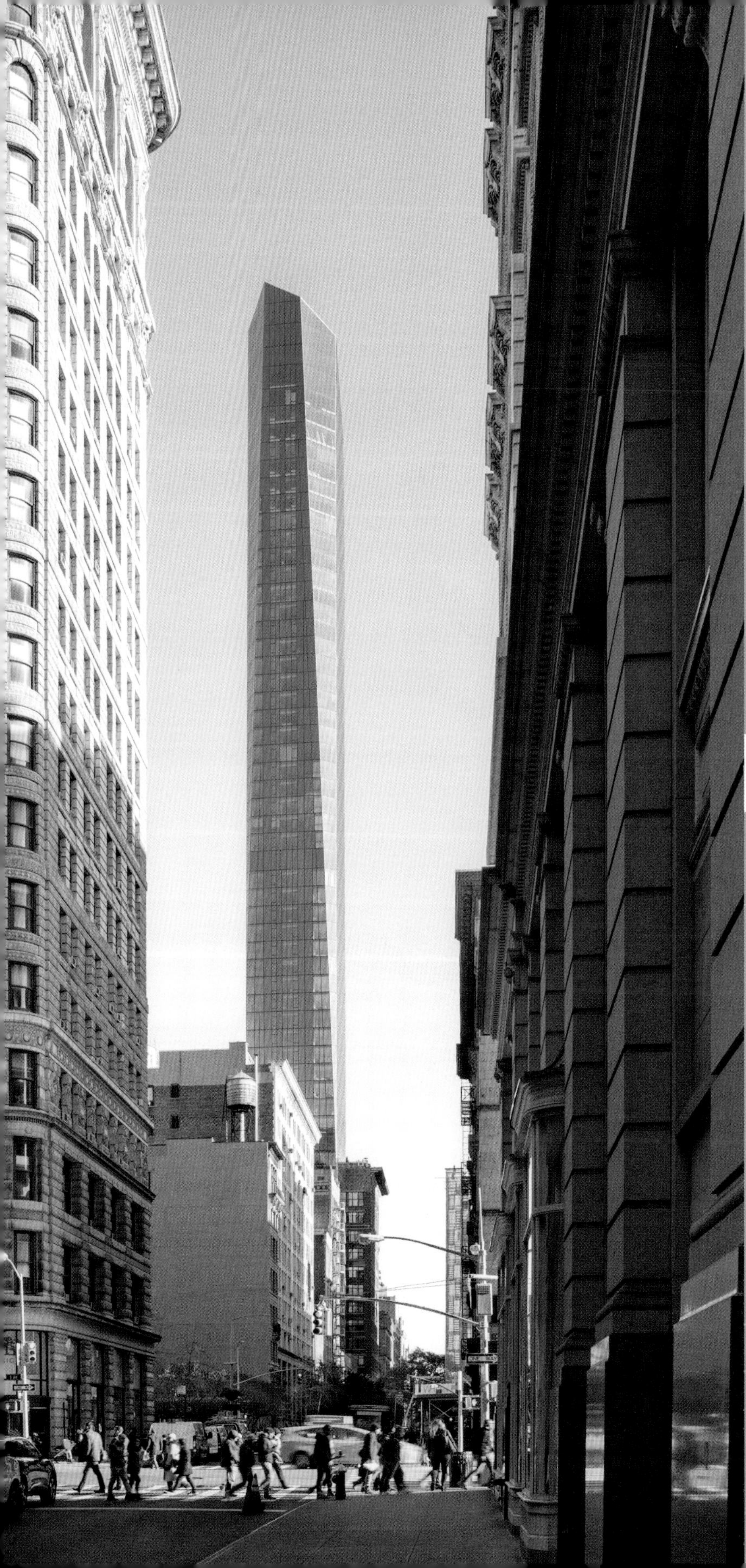

121 East 22nd Street — Cut Corners

044 E

121 East 22nd Street, near
Gramercy Park, Midtown South
*Shohei Shigematsu and Rem Koolhaas of
the Office for Metropolitan Architecture,
OMA, with SLCE Architects*
2018

R **W** **6** to 23 Street

Many buildings in New York are pretty much about what you see from across the street. There is not much going on beyond their facades and whatever the architect wanted to say is all there, on the surface. There are just three types of buildings that make up any city — freestanding, those with a single facade, and corner buildings. There are, of course, hybrids, and in a way, every building is a hybrid. 121 East 22nd Street is a corner- and single-facade hybrid. The 18-story residential building sits at the intersection of Lexington Avenue and 23rd Street, near Gramercy Park, and features a striking three-dimensional prismatic corner with a setback at the 13th floor, and an inner courtyard. The building's namesake address refers to a small, 13-story portion of the development that opens on 22nd Street with a single facade and entrance lobby, while the entire ground floor on the more prominent 23rd Street side is reserved for commerce. It is a fascinating self-conflicting work that reflects its architect's struggle to choose between being either contextual or original. The more you move your eyes away from the neighbors — stone, prewar buildings — the more the architect's individuality is expressed. This individuality is restricted to experiments with such issues as materiality and depth along the plane facades, and is manifested more fully in a series of bird's-mouths that climb up the corner to allow for uniquely framed street and city views for those few who occupy these corner apartments and any pedestrian strolling by. In our 2018 interview with Shohei Shigematsu, leading partner at OMA New York and the building's designer, the Fukuoka-born architect explained, "This building was designed for the site with confused, almost schizophrenic identity due to its prominent location on a busy commercial street and yet, in close proximity to two parks — Gramercy and Madison Square. The idea was to turn this confusion into our concept. It is a stitched corner. As it is the first ground-up OMA building in New York, I didn't want it to be overtly expressive. The building is restrained, contextual, and purposely not personal."

5

Images: OMA by Encore

Prism Tower — Crystal
400 Park Ave South,
Midtown South
Christian de Portzamparc
2016

045 D 045 D

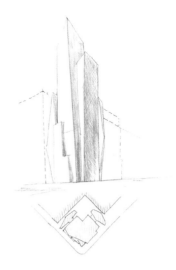

Drawing by Christian de Portzamparc

R W 6 to 28 Street

Despite being known for his many innovative music centers built all over the world, Paris-based architect Christian de Portzamparc's work in New York has focused exclusively on designing towers, all clad in glass (three are included in this book). Locked into a corner of Park Avenue South and 28th Street, and surrounded mostly by early-20th-century stone buildings, this 40-story prismatic glass structure of multiple spikes and folds, is meant to gather light and optimize street views. It is marketed as a living artwork, and based on the building's sculptural form alone, it would be silly to deny this. The bottom 22 floors consist of rental apartments accessed from 28th Street, while the top 18 floors are reserved for condominiums that have their own access on Park Avenue South. Even though the rental tenants and condo residents share the lower level amenities, different companies developed them. In our 2016 interview at the architect's Paris studio, Portzamparc said: "In my residential complex on Rue des Hautes Formes, built in 1979 in Paris, I tried to break away from the anonymous character of architecture. In that first residential project, if I had several types of windows, it was a challenge for my contractor. Ten to 15 years later I could have as many variations as I wanted; it was no longer a challenge. And now almost anything is possible!" He went on, "When I draw or paint, I don't try to reason my moves and preferences. It is not always necessary to tell why certain things are designed the way they are designed. Language becomes important when I involve my team to communicate my ideas and develop projects. Architecture cannot be reduced to language. Language is about communication, but space is about presence, a primitive, ancient, and archaic way to relate to the world and express how we see it. Architecture can communicate because it goes beyond language."

Photos: Wade Zimmerman

5

262 Fifth Avenue — Needle
262 Fifth Avenue,
Midtown South
Yuri Grigoryan of Meganom
2020

046 D

R W 6 to 28 Street

"A room over the city" was the design vision for each of about 40 apartments stacked into a strikingly skinny 54-story tower on its way to reaching the magical height of 1,001 feet (305 meters) at the corner of Fifth Avenue and 29th Street. The building is the first New York project by Moscow-based architect Yuri Grigoryan, the leading partner of Meganom. The building's plan forms two linked rectangles extruded straight up. One is a monolithic service core-spine, with elevators, stairs, and all the necessary mechanical and communications shafts. The other is basically a container of spaces, with clean, column-free, and completely flexible interiors. The building's single-floor apartments, as well as duplexes and one triplex at the top, are suspended like "shelves in the air" and supported only on the east and west sides, while leaving north and south free of any structural support and open to expansive views with the Empire State Building just a few blocks to the north and the Flatiron Building to the south. The tower is topped by a distinctive, covered

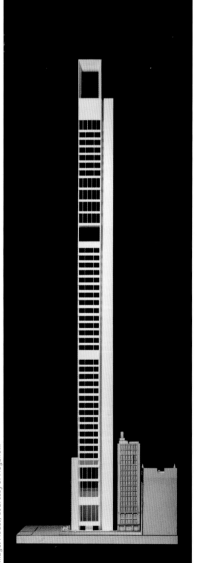

Image: Model, Courtesy of Meganom

Image: DBOX, Courtesy of Meganom

observation deck pavilion that is open to all tenants and their guests. This iconic top echoes the slit at the end of a needle. Once fully built, the building will join a number of recently-built, super-slim towers around Madison Square Park, including another 55-story tower, Rafael Viñoly's residential building a block away at the corner of Fifth Avenue and 30th Street. Here is an excerpt from my 2016 conversation with Grigoryan during one of his frequent visits to New York: "My goal in architecture is to find the right type of building, in changing the actual archetype or inventing an entirely new type. This process of finding the right type is the most interesting part to me. Today, building types constantly pulsate, mutate, and lead to new hybrid types. The goal is to find the most straightforward solution. Yet, any realization is the intermediate phase. Architecture is not simply utilitarian or functional. Many buildings go through reincarnations and change their purpose many times. Architecture is interesting because forms or so-called shells can be filled with various functions over time. This is the goal of an architect — to create a kind of form that would correspond to different functions. Any form is artistic. All buildings are made up. They illustrate either one thing or another. The meaning and purpose of architecture is in inventing a form, but not just a new form. Such a form should be local and specific."

5

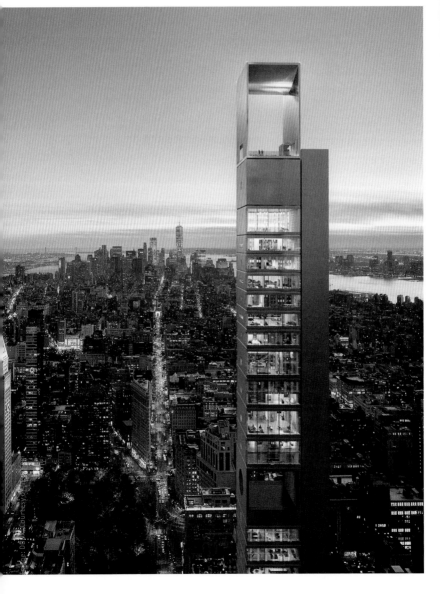

Morgan Library — Piazza

225 Madison Avenue, Midtown
*Renzo Piano Building Workshop
with Beyer Blinder Belle*
2006

047 D

Ⓑ Ⓓ Ⓕ Ⓜ Ⓝ Ⓠ Ⓡ Ⓦ
to 34 Street-Herald Square
Ⓖ to 33 Street
④ ⑤ ⑦ and *Metro-North* to Grand Central

Renzo Piano's work is about many things, but it would be a stretch to call it "iconic," as far as his buildings' resemblance to particular images is concerned, yet this guide includes three buildings designed by the architect. This is partially because of Piano's own iconic status and partially due to the significance of the institutions that are housed in these buildings. Piano is known in the U.S. as a museum architect, having built one in just about every major American city. When he was asked to take part in a small, by-invitation competition to redesign the new Morgan Library he declined, signaling that if the client wanted his input he should hire him directly. It is now widely acknowledged that his being hired directly was the right choice. The Morgan Library is a complex of buildings, an urban village, designed in different styles over a period of over 150 years. It includes J.P. Morgan Jr.'s 1853 Italianate-style mansion at the corner of Madison Avenue and 37th Street, the 1906 library designed by Charles McKim in the Italian Renaissance style along

36th Street, and the 1928 annex building that replaced J.P. Morgan's 19th-century home at the corner of Madison Avenue and 36th Street. Following the acquisition of J.P. Morgan Jr.'s mansion by the Library in 1988, a garden court—a glass-enclosed conservatory designed by New York-based architect Bart Voorsanger—was constructed in 1991 to link the three historical buildings. Piano cleared Voorsanger's addition and inserted three graceful, minimalist pavilions clad in off-white painted steel panels along the perimeter. These pavilions include the new entrance with additional gallery space, and a reading room above. The entrance was shifted to the more prominent Madison Avenue side, away from sleepy 36th Street. Several floors of offices and service areas were placed along 37th Street, and a small cube-shape gallery between the original library and the Annex landed on 36th Street. The bulk of the new addition—book vaults, a theater, amenities—were placed deep underground by blasting through 50 feet (15 meters) of bedrock. This freed up room for the soaring ground floor, a piazza-like court space that sits under a new large glass roof, and through which some nearby towers, including the Empire State Building, can be seen. Note the two hydraulic elevators with their exposed machinery, and a gorgeous stair going underground. This seems to be nothing special

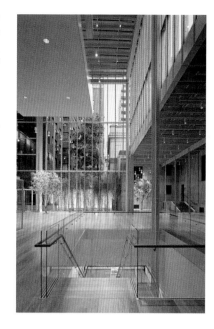

until you pay attention to the absolutely minimal support system and the beautiful details that make the structure stable enough with the use of the thinnest steel parts possible. As a young architect, I was once designing a similar stair, connecting three office floors. I carefully measured the Morgan stair and challenged my engineer with, "This is the kind of stair I want." He replied, "There is not enough meat to hold it up. It will never work." You can see the structure for yourself at this museum. God is in the details!

Photos: Denancé Michel

American Copper Buildings — Letter K
626 First Avenue, Murray Hill
SHoP Architects
2017

048 D

6 to 33 Street

Originally, this attention-grabbing pair of towers was named quite innocuously, 626 First Avenue. The complex is now known as the American Copper Buildings due to the 5,000 copper panels that clad the facades in a manner that is similar to other works by SHoP, such as the Barclays Center and 9 DeKalb Avenue, both in Brooklyn. On its website, the skyscraper's dual towers (one is 540 feet [165 meters], the other 470 feet [143 meters]) are advertised as being, "the new skyline icon of New York."

They bend in the middle to meet at a skybridge, echoing a pair of dancers holding hands. However, the buildings' profile looks more easily identifiable as a letter H or K, depending on how you look at it. The skybridge, which connects the two towers 300 feet (92 meters) from the ground, holds three floors of amenities, including a residents' lounge and a swimming pool. It is also topped with private terraces. In our 2013 interview, Gregg Pasquarelli, one of SHoP's founding partners, said: "To us, one of the key questions is how the building is made and how pieces are put together, and how to make the building live and breathe in the most positive way. When you allow all of those things to come together, what happens is that sometimes the resulting building looks differently from what the expectation may be."

5

Manhattan: Midtown North

Midtown, Theater District, Roosevelt Island

6

057 432 Park Avenue

051 Bank of America Tower

060 One57

049 New York Times Building

6

New York Times Building — Hatch

6

New York Times Building —
Hatch
620 Eighth Avenue, Midtown
Renzo Piano Building Workshop
with FXFOWLE Architects
2007

 049 D

A C E to 42 Street-Port Authority
Bus Terminal

While discussing Renzo Piano's Morgan Library, I already mentioned that his architecture can be called many things but not "iconic." What proves that point better than his design for 52-story tower, located right in the heart of New York, which houses perhaps the most iconic institution in the city's history, the New York Times? The building's image, though elegant and refined, recalls nothing in particular. It seems to dissolve into pure air without having much of an outline. The steel-framed building, cruciform in plan, features four independently floating facade screens, distinguished by closely-spaced horizontal lines of white ceramic rods that echo lines on a hatched drawing. The tower stands between 40th and 41st Streets, along Eighth Avenue, directly across from the Port Authority

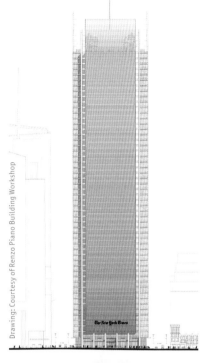

Bus Terminal. Its roof ends 748 feet (228 m) above the street, while its four facade screens extend 92 feet (28 m) higher to 840 feet (260 m), and a central mast rises to 1,046 feet (319 m), which ties with the Chrysler Building, just seven blocks to the east. The ceramic rods are 1 5/8 inches (41.3 mm) in diameter; their spacing increases from the lower floors to the top, adding transparency as the building rises. The rods maximize light and views, while providing privacy and sun shading. They also appear to change color with the sun and weather, acting as an aesthetic veil. The steel framing and bracing is exposed at the building's four corner notches. In the of summer 2008, just one year after the tower was finished, three people climbed its external facade within a month of each other, the first two on the same day. Soon after the building's management removed some of the low-level rods, and since there was another attempt to climb the building in 2012, more rods were removed. They now start at the third floor.

Drawing: Courtesy of Renzo Piano Building Workshop

6

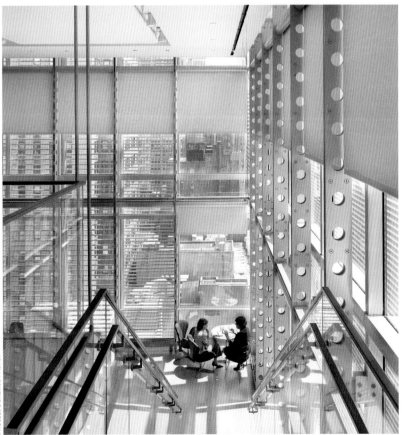

Photos: Denancé Michel

7 Bryant Park — Hourglass
1045 Avenue of the Americas,
Midtown
*Henry Cobb of Pei Cobb Freed
& Partners*
2014

050 D

B D F M to 42 Street-Bryant Park
7 to 5 Avenue

7 Bryant Park's original owner, Hines, proudly described this building as a trophy-class office tower. Situated on Avenue of the Americas between West 39th and 40th Streets, diagonally across from the southwest corner of Bryant Park, the building was designed by Henry Cobb of Pei Cobb Freed & Partners. The steel-and-glass 30-story tower is made up of two rectangular prisms, a lower one of nine stories and the top one of 21 stories, and is distinguished by its carved, conical corner, an unexpected solution that challenges the familiar wedding cake office building design. Two conical incisions sit point-to-point on top of each other in an arrangement that resembles an uneven hourglass or a twisted bow tie. The building would be fairly original if it was not for its predecessor, Tour PB6, a 40-story tower in the La Défense business district of Paris also designed by Cobb, and built back in 2001. While the Paris version features only the lower carved conical corner, it is more elegant than the Manhattan edition, as that tower avoids the use of rectilinear geometry entirely and assumes a more sculptural expression. Both buildings create generous pedestrian plazas accentuated by discus-shaped circular canopies; however, the one in Manhattan is notably less generous. Still, the building offers a much-welcomed alternative to the typical 90-degree, solid street corner we are so accustomed to in New York City and other downtowns across the country.

Photos: Alex Fradkin

Bank of America Tower — Icicle 051 D

One Bryant Park, Midtown
Cook + Fox Architects
2009

🅑🅓🅕🅜 to 42 Street-Bryant Park
🄽 to 5 Avenue

The 55-story Bank of America Tower at One Bryant Park is the headquarters for Bank of America's operations in New York City. It is located on Sixth Avenue between 42nd and 43rd Streets. Its icicle-like crystal form of glass, steel, and aluminum rises to the height of 1,200 feet (366 meters), including a 255-foot (78-meter) architectural spire. At the time the building was built it was the second tallest structure in New York, after the Empire State Building. The faceted crystal design features unique sculptural surfaces with crisp folds and precise vertical lines that are animated by the movement of the sun. The base incorporates a through-block passageway, an urban garden room, an entrance pavilion for the subway, and the Henry Miller Theatre with its restored Georgian-style original facade and reception room rebuilt on 43rd Street. The tower was designed to be the world's most environmentally advanced high-rise office building when such sophisticated technologies were a novelty, with a particular emphasis on water efficiency, indoor air quality, and energy efficiency. To that end, some of the features were pushed to absurd extremes. For example, a tiny lawn on the roof is advertised as a feature that reduces the urban heat island effect. The lack of a garage is presented as having a positive effect on the environment. Meanwhile tens of thousands of cars pass the building daily, looking for parking.

One Vanderbilt — Ziggurat 052 D
1 Vanderbilt Avenue, Midtown
James von Klemperer of
Kohn Pedersen Fox
2020

B D F M to 42 Street-Bryant Park
4 5 6 7 and *Metro-North*
to Grand Central

One Vanderbilt has been described as "an unforgettable landmark" by its designer, James von Klemperer, president and design principal of Kohn Pedersen Fox. It was made possible by the rezoning of East Midtown, which was initiated by former mayor Michael Bloomberg, that passed under Mayor Bill de Blasio. Located immediately to the west of Grand Central Station on 42nd Street, the new tower will reach the height of 1,401 feet (427 meters). It is set to drive up the neighborhood's current, already much-to-be-avoided level of density to something that will be quite unprecedented, making this stretch of 42nd Street perhaps the densest place on Earth. Formally, the building's massing is comprised of four interlocking and tapering volumes that spiral up and evoke a sky-high ziggurat. One of its terraces, at a height of 1,020 feet (311 meters), will house an indoor-outdoor observation deck. This super-tall building will join two nearby icons, the Empire State Building and the Chrysler Building, to comprise a trio of sculptural towers that share one-point connections with the sky, a commendable tradition rooted in the design of pointy-topped cupolas, minarets, spires, and turrets. One Vanderbilt is representative of the way our city manages to improve the quality of the public realm and transportation access in exchange for allowing private enterprise to maximize profits. In this case, not only was the building's height negotiated through a purchase of air rights over Grand Central Station, but the building's developer was also required to invest $220 million in a pedestrian plaza on Vanderbilt Avenue, and to pay for improvements to subway entrances, stairs, and the station below.

Image: Courtesy of Kohn Pedersen Fox

TKTS — Stoop
Father Duffy Square
in Times Square, between
46th and 47th Streets,
Theater District
CHROFI with Perkins Eastman
2008

053 D

N R W to 49 Street
1 to 50 Street

Designed by Sydney-based John Choi, Tai Ropiha, and Steven Fighera, the founding partners of the architecture firm CHROFI, the TKTS ticketing booth that occupies the north end of Times Square was a result of an international competition that attracted almost 700 entries from over 30 countries. The firm's proposal consisted of a tiered, red glass staircase that rises a couple of dozen steps upward to provide both a roof for the booth and what has proved to be a popular public gathering and Instagram-perfect space above. The stair platform is lit from within by LEDs, generating a powerful glow at night that feels at home in the company of the myriad oversized advertising screens that desperately compete for attention. Despite this stoop-like structure's modest size, it has become one of Times Square's most iconic features over the last decade.

6

Photos: John Saeyong

6

11 East 52nd Street, Midtown
Raimund Abraham
2002

054 D

🅔 Ⓜ to 5 Avenue-53 Street
🌀 to 51 Street

I remember that in 1996, when almost nothing was being built in New York, the Austrian-born New York architect, Raimund Abraham (1933–2010), was enthusiastically introducing his Cooper Union students, me among them, to his just-published book *(Un)Built*. One particular section was devoted to the daring tower of the Austrian Cultural Forum. The project won a 1992 international competition. Hosted by the Republic of Austria, the prestigious competition attracted 226 entries from Austrian-born architects. The winning scheme was chosen over entries by such acclaimed architects as Viennese Hans Hollein and Sydney-based Harry Seidler. Back then, the promise of the building's potential realization was viewed as the embodiment of hope that more experimental architecture would be constructed in New York. The Forum is the most prominent project realized by Abraham, whose only other built work in New York is the 1989 Anthology Film Archives on the Lower East Side. He was more known for visionary unbuilt projects with such titles as "Houses without Rooms" and "Seven Gates to Eden." In our 2002 interview, the architect told me: "What I mean by radical is the ability to offer resistance to what is obvious... People have lost the will to resist things, to resist fashions, and to resist the unhesitating admiration of everything that's new. We need to call into question the actual roots of the language and thereby to come up with a new grammar, a new etymology." The new tower occupies a mid-block site, just 25 feet wide (7.5 meters), which was formerly the Forum's five-story townhouse. The new building rises 24 stories, with the authority of a landmark. The tower's sharp-edged architecture with its layered mask-like facade and tilting "slicing blades" of zinc and glass is often compared to a guillotine. The architect preferred to liken it to an Easter Island head. The facade leans back diagonally as it rises and is actually set to the angle described by New York City's building-envelope code; most buildings satisfy this by using more conventional straightforward setbacks. The tower's vertically-stacked rooms contain many functions: galleries, a lecture hall, a library, loft-like presentation and seminar rooms, offices, and a three-level residence for the Forum's director. These are sandwiched between the front facade and the fire escape stair in a sculptural form that the architect called the building's "vertebra." It can be seen by looking up through a skylight in the back of the main gallery at the ground floor.

6

MoMA addition — City in Miniature

Photo: Courtesy of the Museum of Modern Art.

Manhattan: Midtown North 161

6

MoMA addition —
City in Miniature
11 West 53rd Street, Midtown
Yoshio Taniguchi with KPF
2004

055 D

🄴 🄼 to 5 Avenue-53 Street
🄱 🄳 🄵
to 47–50 Streets-Rockefeller Center

In 1939 Philip Goodwin and Edward Durell Stone positioned the modestly-scaled original Museum of Modern Art building midblock on the north side of West 53rd Street between Fifth and Sixth Avenues. It was then populated by opulent, gorgeous Beaux-Arts brownstones. The museum never stopped growing and its entire history is intrinsically tied to multiple demolitions that destroyed most of the block's original architecture. Interestingly, it is also true that these expansions are the reason this stretch of West 53rd Street is the city's most nuanced, and richest block, both historically and architecturally. There is nothing like it — both sides of the block are lined up practically back-to-back with buildings designed by top international architects: from towers by Eero Saarinen, Kevin Roche, Cesar Pelli, and Jean Nouvel to buildings and interiors by Stone, Isamu Noguchi, Philip Johnson, Yoshio Taniguchi, and Enrique Norten. The block continues to reinvent itself and sometimes even buildings distinguished by world-class architecture are not able to stop the museum's relentless growth, as was the case when the 13-year-old, beautiful home of the Folk Art Museum by Tod Williams and Billie Tsien was pulled out in 2014 to accommodate the current expansion designed by Diller Scofidio + Renfro. Yoshio Taniguchi's 2004 expansion, just west of the original, was driven by MoMA's lack of room for the display of its continuously growing collection. It even considered moving to a new, more open location, but several buildings adjacent to MoMA were put up for sale. That presented a better option for expanding its existing venue. A long search for the appropriate architect led to a top 10 list with three finalists — Bernard Tschumi, Herzog & de Meuron, and Tokyo-based Taniguchi. The Harvard-educated architect had never built outside of his native Japan before being selected for the job here, but he had a solid reputation as a museum architect, having designed about a dozen Modernist museums in Tokyo, Nagano, Hiroshima, and Kyoto. The main concept here is clear: this is a city in miniature, though Central Park, surrounded on four sides by perfectly lined up stone and glass towers, is perhaps a more direct metaphor, as the museum is composed around its own "Central Park," the Sculpture Garden, originally designed by Philip Johnson and slightly enlarged by Taniguchi. Exploring the museum is reminiscent of navigating Manhattan itself; the building "breathes" freely and the higher you climb, the greater excitement you feel. Small footbridges with glass parapets thrown between the sixth-floor slabs, under the atrium's glass ceiling, are particularly impressive. If coming to the glass doesn't put butterflies in your stomach, nothing will. When it was

Taniguchi's turn to address the hundreds of journalists at the museum's inauguration press conference, the architect was brief. "I have nothing to tell you — just come and look." He also famously said: "If you give me enough money, I'll design you a beautiful building. If you give me a lot of money, I'll make it disappear." The architect was given a lot of money, and he kept his word. Architecture does disappear here, but not because there is nothing to talk about: it is just understated, or one could say, composed of numerous laboriously understated details. As a result, MoMA's architecture fades into the background. Yet, it comes into an acute focus when one climbs elegant stairs, transitions from one space to another, or suddenly catches a glimpse of a particular urban pocket that may look no less inspiring than art on display. I wonder what Taniguchi's friend, Japanese architect Fumihiko Maki meant when he told me at the opening that the new building looked, like "London in New York." I think he referred to the fact that New York was finally getting modernized in distinctly visual terms. Perhaps the adjective that is the most appropriate for MoMA is impressive. It impresses you with its size, sophistication, and spatial grandeur. It is a reasonably efficient machine for bringing people together, which is what art museums are. The new MoMA is the modern mega museum as cultural icon, social center, status symbol, tourist attraction, art mall, and high-end shopping opportunity; it is all of the above, and despite the ballooned scale and ever-growing crowds, it is still a place where art can be experienced as spiritual retreat. Here is an excerpt from my 2006 interview with Stephen Rustow, then a design principal at Kohn Pedersen Fox (KPF), who were the executive architects for the expansion: "At first glance, Taniguchi's use of formal vocabulary seems to be anchored in a completely conventional syntax and a familiar set of modernist tropes, yet it is full of elegant subtleties and unintended contradictions, which render it more complex and ambiguous than the casual viewer might suppose. As a result, you are faced with architecture much more concerned with pure sensual effect, creating a kind of libertinism of sublime calm — a minimalist baroque. Whether glass, stone, metal, wood or plaster, every wall, floor, and ceiling are all composed as a perfect isolated surface and detailed to permit no reading of the actual depth of the material itself. Thus, virtually nowhere does a material turn a corner without a frame or a reveal to contain it."

6

E M to 5 Avenue-53 Street
B D F
to 47–50 Streets-Rockefeller Center

Discretely named 53 West 53rd Street, and formerly known as Tower Verre (Glass Tower), this strikingly beautiful skyscraper is located directly across 53rd Street from the CBS Building, also known as Black Rock, which was designed by Eero Saarinen. 53 West 53rd puts its characteristic receding stealth geometry on full display from Sixth Avenue and the through-block plaza directly to the east of the CBS Building. Echoing early-20th-century renderings by Hugh Ferriss, 53 West 53rd Street's angular, faceted silhouette is guided by zoning regulations, and the intent to maximize optimal views of the city. The tower's slenderness is compensated by an exposed structural system, an irregular diagrid designed to withstand high wind loads. I have nicknamed this tower "Nouvel" to honor the Paris-based architect's admirable insistence on bringing art, theater, and delight into the business of building commercial buildings in New York. All of his buildings here prove his utter devotion to experimentation and resistance to mere expedience, frugality, profitability, and predictability.

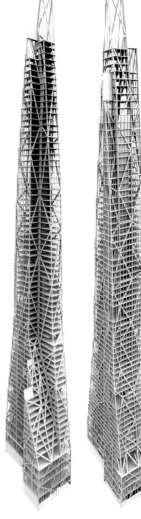

Images: Courtesy of Ateliers Jean Nouvel

This bold, 73-story (for marketing purposes it is advertised as comprising 82 floors) tower culminates in several tapered peaks, which stand 1,050 feet (320 meters) from the top. Initially, the tower was to reach 1,250 feet, or 381 meters (the same height as the Empire State Building minus its mast), but this proposal ran into considerable opposition from the New York City Planning Commission, which focused on fears that it would cast a shadow over Central Park and compete with already established high-rises on the city skyline. The building was given the go-ahead only after the architect agreed to clip 200 feet (61 meters) off its top. It is unfortunate that the original design was blocked. If we agree that New York is a commercially-driven vertical city, we might as well let it grow freely; there is beauty in that. Still, even as cropped, the tower is now visible from afar and it signals the exact location of the Museum of Modern Art below. Now that MoMA has demolished the 13-year-old former home of the American Folk Art Museum, designed by Tod Williams and Billie Tsien, the tower and the museum have become neighbors. Moreover, the condominium's lower floors will be taken over by MoMA's gallery space. Forty-thousand square feet (3,700 square meters) of additional space will connect directly to the museum's double-height second-, fourth- and fifth-floor galleries. It will be interesting to see where MoMA expands next, now that it has started stepping over buildings and going right through them.

6

057 D

6

View of Midtown with 432 Park Avenue

432 Park Avenue — Viñoly
432 Park Avenue, Midtown
Rafael Viñoly
2016

057 D

E M to 5 Avenue-53 Street
N R W to 5 Avenue-59 Street

Standing right in the middle of Manhattan, where Park Avenue is intersected by East 57th Street, 432 Park Avenue is impossible to miss. Designed by Uruguayan-born, New York-based architect Rafael Viñoly, the tower is visible from just about everywhere in the city. The building's literally breakneck height of 1,396 feet (425.5 meters), as it stretches to 96 floors, is dominating, imposing, assertive, and soaring, yet elegant and refreshing. The building is a perfectly square gridded tube, measuring 93 feet (28 meters) on each side, clad in concrete punctuated by 10-foot (3-meter) square windows (only six on each side) is the fitting expression of the Manhattan's orthogonal street grid. It is the tower's height and proportions — its slenderness ratio is 15:1 — that draw the eyes to the sky where it, as yet, has no competition. Midtown Manhattan's dense forest of skyscrapers barely reaches to its waistline. The building is taller than both the Empire State Building and One World Trade Center minus their spires. Proportionally, the tower echoes a pencil, but I think it is more appropriate, in this case, to call it, "Viñoly." The building is daring and provoking; already several other super tall, super slim, and ultra-luxury residential towers along 57th Street and the south end of Central Park, which has been

dubbed Billionaires' Row, are being constructed to reach even higher. For now, most of this slender tower's residences enjoy uninterrupted panoramic views that include Central Park and the rivers. The tower is designed as seven "independent buildings" stacked up, separated by spaces where the building cores are exposed to the outdoors. These breaks allow for the deflection of wind pressure and help achieve structural stability. The six upper volumes, starting 200 feet (61 meters) above grade, contain 54 residential floors that can accommodate from one to four residential units. The lowest section of the tower contains such amenities as meeting rooms, a screening room, restaurant, spa, fitness center, swimming pool, wine cellars, and underground parking. During a 2007 conversation at Viñoly's New York studio, almost a decade before 432 Park Avenue made him a household name, the architect shared with me his views on building high: "I think it is hard not to have a position or philosophy about tall buildings while living and practicing architecture in a city like New York," he said. "It is a unique urban experience. The basic planning strategy — the grid — is probably the most ingenious planning device anywhere in the world. The genius of the grid is in the fact that it absorbs all possible growth and maintains the right balance. The city is not shaped by aesthetical decisions. It works like an incredible mechanism and there is no conflict in losing unity because it is in this perpetual mode of evolving. Everything is very pragmatic and there is beauty and harmony in that too."

6

LVMH Tower — Flower
19 East 57th Street, Midtown
Christian de Portzamparc
1999

E M to 5 Avenue-53 Street
N R W to 5 Avenue-59 Street

Drawing: by Christian de Portzamparc

Built in 1999, this visually attractive, if not quite stunning by today's standards, building is the U.S. headquarters of LVMH. Standing at a mere 24 stories, this handsomely sculpted glass tower could hardly be called a skyscraper. Yet, at the time it was a crucial disrupter, bringing world-class architecture to the streets of New York. The building was among the very first signs of a returning interest in bringing contemporary architecture back to a city where local architects, developers, institutions, and city government had dismissed it as artsy and trivial for too long. Located on East 57th Street near Madison Avenue, the building was designed by Paris-based architect Christian de Portzamparc. The building's geometry evokes feminine lines, and at the time, *Architecture* magazine even portrayed it as an evening dress on its cover. The architect himself cites unfolding petals of a flower as inspiration. The facade features angled folds and creases with green-colored, clear, and sandblasted milky white glass panels. Portzamparc's elegant glass creation, built in contrast to the mostly stone buildings around it, received widespread praise from the most demanding architecture critics who showered it with such compliments as "the epitome of controlled, refined elegance," "a stunning, lyrical building," and even, "the best new building in New York — not by small degrees but by the equivalent of a jump shot to the moon." The tower with a setback occurring at the 11th floor, includes a ground-level store space for Christian Dior, designed by New York-based architect Peter Marino, and is topped by a glass-enclosed, cube-shaped penthouse used for receptions, with a 30-foot-high (nine-meter) ceiling. During a 2016 interview with Portzamparc at his Paris office, the architect told me, "Every project is a step-by-step process. It does not come from above like a dream, although there are exceptions and I did have one of my projects come to me in a dream... but for LVMH it started with a very narrow site, then the client purchased an adjacent site and our dimensions doubled. There were many zoning conditions I had to respond to. But my biggest concern was the giant IBM Tower directly across the street, which is covered in gray-green glass and polished granite. So, if I also had a straight glass facade my building would simply reflect the IBM and disappear. That's why I wanted to break the line of the facade into facets and also to use sanded, translucent glass to avoid mirroring the building across the street. So, as you can see, so-called inspirations often come from local difficulties, which I found was a challenge. Other things may exist that I am not really conscious of. For me inspirations are about responding to the specifics."

Photo: Wade Zimmerman

111 West 57th Street — Feather 059 D
111 West 57th Street, Midtown
SHoP Architects
2020

F to 57 Street
B D E to 7 Avenue
N Q R W to 57 Street-7 Avenue

111 West 57th Street, is also referred to as the Steinway Tower because it incorporates the original landmarked 1925 Steinway Hall building designed by Warren & Wetmore, the architects of the Grand Central Station and the Helmsley Building. Aiming to become the tallest building in Midtown, it is an 82-story supertall residential skyscraper that will rise to 1,428 feet (435 meters). It is not just the height that attracts attention: with a width-to-height ratio of about 1:24, its extreme thinness is remarkable. Just looking at it can be terrifying, and it feels that it may snap any second. It appears to be as thin and fragile as a feather. Yet, the tower's stability will be perfectly balanced by an 800-ton tuned mass damper that will work its magic and reduce the amplitude of harmonic vibrations in the case of high winds or seismic events. The north side of the tower rises directly up to its pinnacle, while on the south side, it cascades downward in a dozen blade-like setbacks. As the height of the building increases, the setbacks eventually thin out and the tower

literally "disappears into the sky." Look up and try to count the number of floors — it is quite impossible, as the building's facades are resolved in a series of vertical bands finished in terracotta, bronze, and glass that create a sweeping play of shadow and light. A glass curtain wall on the north facade takes full advantage of the tower's front and center views of Central Park, as the building occupies a near-perfect spot centered right on it. In my 2013 interview with SHoP's founding partner Gregg Pasquarelli, he pointed out the following: "We stay away from ever imposing an object on a place. We always start with the following question — what is the logic of how the building has to work? What will make the performance of the program work the best? Then the building, which is being designed, is placed into an environment. That environment has flows, positions, connections... When that happens does the building hit the site like a rock? Or does it move and connect in many different ways? These are the questions we face to better resolve its performance."

6

One57 — Waterfall
157 West 57th Street, Midtown
Christian de Portzamparc
2014

060 D

🄵 to 57 Street
🄱 🄳 🄴 to 7 Avenue
🄽 🄠 🅁 🅆 to 57 Street-7 Avenue

The early-20th-century American architect and writer Claude Bragdon saw skyscrapers as the embodiment of the idea of arrested upward motion; an image of a frozen fountain. He wrote, "For structural truth and symbolic significance, there should be upward sweeping lines to dramatize the engineering fact of vertical continuity and the poetic fancy of an ascending force in resistance to gravity — a fountain." Nowadays, of course, towers have all kinds of ways to get to the top, including a loop, as in the case of Rem Koolhaas' CCTV skyscraper in Beijing. Still, fountains and waterfalls naturally serve as obvious inspirations for a soaring tower. Designed by Christian de Portzamparc, One57 is quite literally inspired by a waterfall: from its Gustave Klimt-like pixilation of multicolored glass panels cascading from the building's top, to the splashes of wavy bands of polished metal turning into canopies over the sidewalk, the tower's lines express the energy of falling water. The 75-story skyscraper, that stands at 1,005 feet (306 meters) tall, springs out of an L-shaped site just off the corner of Seventh Avenue and 57th Street, which is often referred to as

the Billionaire's Row for its recent accumulation of super-tall towers for the super-rich. In our 2017 interview, conducted at Portzamparc's Paris studio, the architect noted: "I never stopped perceiving space as an artistic medium. I understood that no one else but an architect could solve the problems of the contemporary city. Reinventing is a very pretentious position. Instead, we recreate things through an intense dialogue between generations and ideas. We start again. We live in an era of constant change and willingly or unwillingly architecture reinvents tomorrow from project to project. I believe that the best projects are about reinventing this confidence in the future."

Photo: Andrea Cau/Unsplash

Apple Store — Glass Cube   `061` `D`
767 5th Avenue, Midtown
Eight Inc., 2006;
Bohlin Cywinski Jackson, 2011;
Foster + Partners, 2018

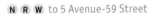 **N** **R** **W** to 5 Avenue-59 Street

"An iconic glass cube rises up from a broad public plaza," says the website of the cube's architect, Wilkes-Barre, Pennsylvania-based firm, Bohlin Cywinski Jackson. Open around the clock every day of the year, the distinctive, minimalist 32-foot (9.8-meter) glass cube is centered on-axis with Edward Durrell Stone's striped 50-story General Motors Building at Fifth Avenue between East 58th and East 59th Streets, which visually anchors the southeast corner of Central Park. The Fifth Avenue Apple glass cube has become to New York what Ise Shrines are to Japan. If the old shrines are dismantled and new ones rebuilt to exacting specifications every 20 years, it seems the Apple Cube is rebuilt every time the newest glass technology makes a sleeker appearance possible. Entirely free of structural steel, the glass cube has served as both the entry portal and iconographic symbol of the underground store. It is self-supporting through the seamless integration of tall glass panels and interconnected glass fins and beams. Housed within the transparent cube is the first structural-glass spiral staircase and glass cylindrical elevator. The light-gathering cube is a perfect representation of the architecture of nothingness, which is consistent with Apple's gadgets whose functionality is completely disguised, elevating the power of technology to pure magic. The glass cube is one of the most photographed structures in New York and is a perfect architectural embodiment of Apple's perfectionistic aesthetic. In fact, Apple's drive to simplify the functionality of its products is reflected in the evolution of the cube. The original cube, built in 2006, was put together out of 90 medium-size glass panels. It was designed by San Francisco-based Eight Inc. The 2011 Bohlin Cywinski Jackson version was streamlined so it used only 15 much larger glass panels. Both firms are responsible for numerous Apple stores around the world. Ever since completing its spaceship-like corporate headquarters in Cupertino, California, designed by Foster + Partners, Apple seems to prefer to hire the British firm for its key projects. In 2017, the cube was dismantled once again. While the store remains open, it is undergoing a significant renovation that will more than double the original size to accommodate its immense popularity. As I write this, the cube is being rebuilt according to the design by Foster + Partners, although no details would be revealed either by Apple or Foster.

6

Photo: Courtesy of Pelli Clarke Pelli Architects

Bloomberg Tower — Keyhole **062 D**
731 Lexington Avenue, Midtown
Cesar Pelli of
Pelli Clarke Pelli Architects
2005

4 5 6 to 59 Street
N R W to Lexington Avenue-59 Street

Known informally as the Bloomberg Tower, because it houses the headquarters of the business information giant, 731 Lexington Avenue takes over a full block, standing between Lexington and Third Avenues and 58th and 59th Streets. Designed by Argentina-born American architect Cesar Pelli, the complex includes restaurants and luxury condominiums. There is also a retail section, separated by a six-story atrium called Beacon Court, a dramatic midblock outdoor public space that contains multiple formal entries, and a *porte cochère*. Elliptical in plan and conical in shape, the court looks like a keyhole from above. The main tower, which is shifted to the west along Lexington Avenue, stands 55 stories tall, reaching 806 feet (246 meters). Despite its respectable height, the building's form is quite conventional. More to the point, it does not have a characteristic "skyscraper top," the feature that had made Pelli famous, particularly in his iconic designs for the World Financial Center in New York, and the Petronas Towers in

Kuala Lumpur, Malaysia. When I visited the architect at his New Haven office in 2005, he told me: "I believe that those buildings that pursue the Miesian flat-topped vision are not skyscrapers. They are high-rise buildings. Mies very strongly did not want his buildings to be called skyscrapers. He called them high-rises and he was right because skyscrapers convey other values and meanings that he was not interested in. A skyscraper is a symbolic thing. But for such a rational architect as Mies it was an anathema. And indeed, there shouldn't be too many skyscrapers. If a building is not the tallest in a particular city, it is fine to be a high-rise building. It makes sense for most tall buildings to be high-rises. Interestingly enough, all of Mies' buildings fit very well. They are very well placed and proportioned. But just a few blocks away from the Seagram Building in New York," Pelli continued, "you don't know which one it is. It is lost. Yet, many blocks away, from a train coming to New York, from Long Island City, or from the New York airports, you can see the Chrysler Building or the Empire State Building. You know where they are and what places they mark in the city. You see the Chrysler Building and you know that the Grand Central Station is right there. It is very important. So, for me any building that pretends to be a skyscraper needs to be quite a bit taller than the buildings around it."

Franklin D. Roosevelt Four
Freedoms Park Memorial —
Exclamation Point
063 D
Southern tip of Roosevelt Island
*Louis Kahn, 1974; Mitchell/Giurgola
Architects executive architect*
2012

🄵 to Roosevelt Island
Roosevelt Island Tramway, Astoria Ferry

Photo: Paul Warchol

Can a work of architecture designed in 1974 be regarded as contemporary? Yes. Even though the Franklin D. Roosevelt Four Freedoms Park Memorial was conceived over 40 years ago, the will — and perhaps a deep need on the part of the public to make it a reality — took place in our time and that's why it was included in this book of more recent iconic structures. The memorial celebrates the Four Freedoms speech (freedom of speech, freedom of faith, freedom from want, and freedom from fear) that Roosevelt articulated in his 1941 State of the Union address. It occupies a four-acre (1.6-hectare) triangular site at the southernmost point of Roosevelt Island, in the East River between Manhattan Island and Queens. The former Welfare Island (its name reflected the fact that starting in 1921 and for decades thereafter it was primarily used for hospitals for the poor) was renamed Roosevelt Island in honor of the late president in 1973, with the intention that his memorial would be built there. The southern part of the island is now being rebuilt as a new Cornell Tech engineering campus, a joint academic venture between Cornell University and the Technion-Israel Institute of Technology. The famed Philadelphia-based Modernist architect Louis Kahn designed the memorial, and this project is his only structure built in New York City. According to Kahn, this "memorial should be a room and a garden," which he chose to be the point of departure in his design approach. These two metaphors, "the garden" as nature and "the room" as the beginning of architecture, echo an exclamation point when seen from above. Kahn completed his drawings for the memorial just before he died at the age of 73 of a heart attack in a restroom at Penn Station, after having just returned from a work trip to India. One-hundred-foot (30-meter)-wide ceremonial stairs lead to the top of the memorial's triangular lawn that tapers down to its tip, leading to the square plaza, hovering slightly above the water level. The lawn is flanked by double rows of little-leaf linden trees that frame views of the New York skyline and harbor, and lead to the 1933 bust of Roosevelt by an American artist, Jo Davidson, who specialized in realistic, intense portraits. The memorial is made entirely in North Carolina granite. Excerpts from Roosevelt's Four Freedoms speech are carved on the memorial's walls.

6

Drawing: Louis I. Kahn Collection, University of Pennsylvania

Manhattan: Uptown

Columbus Circle, Lincoln Center, Upper West Side

065 Time Warner Center

067 Via 57 West

066 Museum of Arts and Design

064 Hearst Tower

Hearst Tower — Bird's-mouths `064 D`
300 West 57th Street,
Upper West Side
Foster + Partners
2006

Ⓐ Ⓑ Ⓒ Ⓓ ❶
to 59 Street-Columbus Circle

The Hearst Tower, by Britain's most re-nowned architect Norman Foster, is a new vision for the 1920s building. Foster's building is placed atop a six-story Art Deco pedestal designed by Joseph Urban and opened in 1929, which was to be the base for a tower, that never materialized. Just steps from Columbus Circle, publish-ing magnate William Randolph Hearst had anticipated this area would become a new media quarter for Manhattan. The new tower by Foster rises above the old build-ing to a height of 46 stories. The interior of the original building was gutted and turned into a huge lobby. Like a bustling town square, this dramatic space pro-vides access to all parts of the building. It incorporates the main elevator lobby, the Hearst staff cafeteria and auditorium, and mezzanine levels for meetings and special functions. Three diagonal esca-lators offset between a cascading fall of chilled water connect the street level en-trance on Eighth Avenue to the grand in-ternal plaza. The two-story high Icefall — a collaboration with New York-based architect-artist James Carpenter and

Photo: Nigel Young/Foster + Partners

Los Angeles-based designer Jim Garland of Fluidity — uses collected rainwater to cool the atrium in summer and humidify in wintertime. *Riverlines*, a colossal, 40-foot by 70-foot (21-meter by 12-meter) installation by British land artist Richard Long is a contemplative mural against the gray stone of the elevator core facing the main entrance. The painting, or "mud work," is created from the mud of the Hudson River and the River Avon near Long's home in England. The artwork, composed of nine strips and entirely made by the artist himself, celebrates the metaphor of the river as a symbol of journey, movement, and life. Unfortunately, due to the heightened security measures in New York after the September 11, 2001 attacks, visitors can only come into a small ground floor lobby but are not allowed to ride the escalators to reach the internal plaza. The triangulated diagrid form is what makes the tower's structure distinctive. Driving north on Eighth Avenue there is a sensation of an optical illusion. The general form is quite arresting and it is not like any other building. Its design suggests vertical growth and continuation. The diagrids form a triangulated truss system that connects all four faces of the tower, creating a highly efficient tube structural system, with inherent lateral stiffness and strength that consumed 20 percent less steel material compared to conventional structures. Eighty-five percent of the steel used here was recycled. The diagrid's nodes are formed by the intersection of the diagonal and horizontal elements, set on a 40-foot per four-floor module. The resulting zigzagging form with corners cut back between the diagonals produces eight-story-high bird's-mouths that form the building's distinctive faceted silhouette. In my 2008 interview with Foster, the architect said: "I think one of the many themes in my work is the benefits of triangulation that can make structures rigid with less material. I think in New York the Hearst Tower gives a kind of urban order. I think the highly repetitive pattern of this tower has a comfortable scale feeling. Buildings like Mies van der Rohe's Seagram tower break scale with elegant bronze mullions in a different way. In the case of the Hearst Tower, it is a very deliberate contrast with the masonry, Art Deco base of the building. I felt this was a good relationship between elements, concepts, styles. Also, the building gives a very strong identity, especially being situated close to Central Park — despite the fact that by New York standards this is a tiny building. So, the symbolic aspect of the building, the technology, and the economic use of materials fuse quite well."

7

7

Time Warner Center —
Twin Towers
10 Columbus Circle
*David Childs of Skidmore,
Owings & Merrill (SOM)*
2003

065 D

Ⓐ Ⓑ Ⓒ Ⓓ ❶
to 59 Street-Columbus Circle

According to the architects' statement, "Time Warner Center, perhaps to a greater extent than any other modern American building, exemplifies the concept of a city within a building, versus a building within a city." This is true, and reminds me of vertical complexes in Asia, particularly in Hong Kong, where a dozen or more different programs are typically tied into an active urban knot. Like those, this complex incorporates a shopping mall, supermarket, restaurants, gyms, spas, office space, an upscale hotel, and residential condominiums. CNN television studios, a jazz venue designed by Rafael Viñoly, and

subway access are also located here. Designed by New York architect David Childs of Skidmore, Owings & Merrill (SOM), the complex occupies the western half of Columbus Circle on a double-block site between 58th and 60th Streets. It is the former site of the New York Coliseum, an exhibition hall built in 1956 and demolished in 2000 to clear space for the current development. Time Warner Center was decades in the making, and the resulting 55-story twin towers are a pitiful version of what was once planned for this site. A series of ambitious competitions organized in the 1980s by the site's owner, the Metropolitan Transportation Authority (MTA), produced some futuristic projects, including a 137-story, 1,600-foot (490-meter)-high building resembling a rocket, proposed by Donald Trump and designed by Israeli-American architect Eli Attia. The project met intense opposition due to concerns about the enormous shadow the highrise would cast over Central Park. In 1988, a New York court ruled that the planned

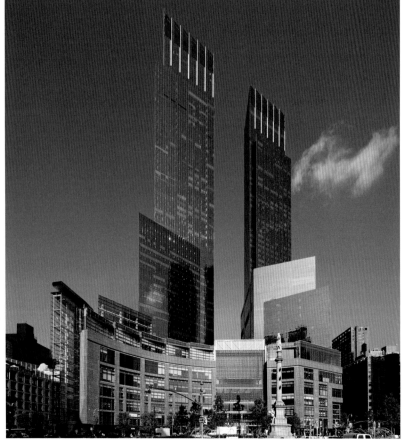

Photo: Jeff Goldberg/Esto

building would violate the city's own zoning ordinances and nullified MTA's sale. The project went dormant. Childs was hired by Related, the complex's developer, to work on various versions of the project from 1988 to 1998. Among his original designs was a building with two towers clad in stone that would stand in one line with five other 1930s Art Deco residential twin towers along Central Park West. What we see today is Child's design, simplified and dressed in glass, a year-2000 version that is more typical of construction today. The center is broken down into a series of setbacks with multiple acute angles and the towers are shaped as parallelograms in plan. Note the razor-sharp southeast corner from which the center appears particularly dynamic. It is from here that the complex opens a strong perspective in all its drama. The opening between the pair of towers is on-axis with Central Park South, so that when one looks at the complex from any point to its east, the building does not appear as a mass

that dead-ends the street just beyond Columbus Circle. The center was already under construction before the September 11 attacks. In 2002, I was among several guests at the press conference organized by Related, at the 53rd floor of Carnegie Tower overlooking Central Park, just a short walk from Columbus Circle. The company's founder and chairman Stephen Ross personally presented the under-construction complex. It was to be the first high-rise built after the destruction of the Twin Towers. As soon as he left the room a couple of journalists impatiently expressed their disbelief at what they were witnessing, saying that Ross was out of touch with reality in his hopes that people were still going to want to live in towers, especially twin towers. But, in fact, it was Ross who could see the future more clearly than most of us. Since then he has initiated a number of other developments, most famously, Hudson Yards, featuring numerous high-rises that are even taller.

7

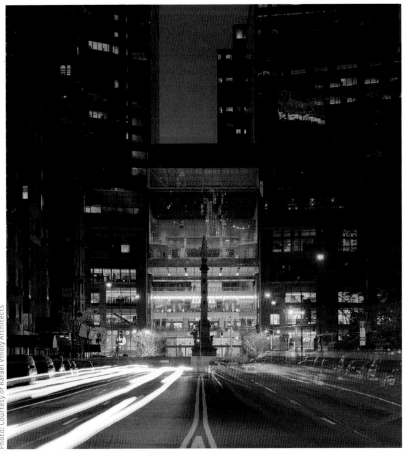

Museum of Arts and Design — Ribbon of Light (formerly Lollipop Building)

2 Columbus Circle
Brad Cloepfil of Allied Works Architecture with Handel Architects
2008

🅐 🅑 🅒 🅓 🅵

to 59 Street-Columbus Circle

Photo: Hélène Binet

Located on a tiny trapezoidal city block facing the southwest corner of Central Park, MAD, the Museum of Arts and Design, (formerly known as the American Craft Museum) designed by Portland- and New York-based architect Brad Cloepfil of Allied Works Architecture is a controversial project, not necessarily because of its appearance, but because it is a renovation and recladding of an existing building that some architectural critics, preservationists, and other well-known New Yorkers thought should have been preserved. The original 1964 building was one of the earliest examples of Postmodernism. It was designed as the Huntington Hartford Gallery of Modern Art by Modernist Edward Durell Stone, known for other prominent New York City buildings such as the Museum of Modern Art and the General Motors Building at the southeast corner of Central Park. The 10-story building's largely solid white marble facade featured an arcaded loggia at the top, decorative perforated panels at its edges, and a colonnaded arcade around its base. It was this ground-floor peculiar detail that won the building its nickname, "the Lollipop Building," a reference to a mocking review by the late *New York Times* architecture critic Ada Louise Huxtable, in which she called it a "die-cut Venetian palazzo on lollipops." The new 12-story iteration is a result of an international competition won by Cloepfil, who was chosen over other finalists including Zaha Hadid. The building is a sleek block finished in textured glazed terra-cotta tile. The building's solidity is rendered with light by the use of continuous two-foot (0.6-meter)-wide ribbons of frosted and clear glass. Radiating from the building's core, they touch every surface — walls, floors, and ceilings — as they move up through the galleries, expanding as they pass through the classroom, office, and restaurant floors. These incisions would look very effective if the building's galleries were to remain empty, but they appear to be quite irrelevant and restrictive to work with when curators must lay out exhibitions. In my interview with Cloepfil at his New York studio in 2008, the architect said about his project: "I wanted it to be one act of architecture — one continuous ribbon of light that would guide you through the volume away from the core along the floor, up the facade wall, then across to bring the natural light in and finally, along the ceiling back to the core. This sequence repeats on each of the four gallery floors. I see the building as a compass point and I wanted people to feel it. For me architecture is not an act of proclamation, but an act of inquiry and investigation. It is not about being contextual, but about investigating what architecture could be — not in terms of form, but in terms of space. We have become so desensitized to things that are not eccentric. I like to think that we are moving towards the post-sensational period of architecture where we would be concerned with meanings, references, and ideas."

Via 57 West — Peak
625 West 57th Street,
Upper West Side
Bjarke Ingels Group (BIG)
2016

Ⓐ Ⓑ Ⓒ Ⓓ ①
to 59 Street-Columbus Circle

Via 57 West, which occupies three quarters of the city block between West 57th and 58th Streets at 12th Avenue, and overlooks the Hudson River in Hell's Kitchen on the West Side, is part of a new generation of architecture. It takes full advantage of what the latest design and building technologies offer in the shaping of highly calculated buildings to address specific locations and programs. Looking at the result, one realizes how flexible and particular our cities can eventually become. This residential building is actually a hyperbolic paraboloid that transitions from a rectangular base into a point in the sky. It is now the most iconic structure on the city's western skyline. What looks like the peak of a warped pyramid is the first finished project in New York by the Danish architecture firm BIG, which moved its main office to the city in 2011. The building is designed as a hybrid between a European-style, low-rise apartment block with a courtyard at the core, and a Manhattan tower, which typically sits on a base. To achieve this effect three corners of the block are kept low and the northeastern corner is lifted up towards its 467-foot (142-meter), 35-story peak. This unusual geometry allows the courtyard apartments to open toward the Hudson and bring the low western sun deep inside the block. The building is one of the few in the city that is all about its form: it is delightfully cinematic, as it shifts constantly, depending on one's vantage point. The building's form or rather its sloping roof, consists of a simple ruled surface punched irregularly by terraces — each one unique and facing south. In our 2009 interview, Bjarke Ingels, then just 35, summarized his firm's teamwork approach by saying: "Our architecture is never triggered by a single event, never conceived by a single mind, and never shaped by a single hand. Neither is it the direct materialization of a personal agenda or pure ideals, but rather the result of an ongoing adaptation to the multiple conflicting forces flowing through society. We, architects don't control the city — we can only aspire to intervene. Architecture evolves from the collision of political, economic, functional, logistical, cultural, structural, environmental, and social interests, as well as interests yet unnamed and unforeseen."

7

Photo: Alex Fradkin

188

Photo: Evan Joseph

Mercedes House — Stairway
550 West 54th Street,
Upper West Side
Enrique Norten of Ten Arquitectos
2012

068 D

C E to 50 Street

Called stunning and iconic by the building's managing team, Mercedes House, designed by New York- and Mexico City-based Enrique Norten of Ten Arquitectos, is a massive 27-story residential and commercial building that occupies most of a city block at the western edge of Midtown. The building is S-shaped in plan, sitting on a three-level rectangular base and rises from De Witt Clinton Park along 11th Avenue eastward, reaching 328 feet (100 meters) at its peak. Each floor of the structure steps up from the one below, allowing for unobstructed views towards the park and the Hudson River, and providing a couple of private roof terraces with green roofs at every floor's southern end. The resulting form of

7

distinctive terraces echoes a cruise ship, appropriately so, as the building directly faces several piers of the Manhattan Cruise Terminal. On the 11th Avenue side, the building's base incorporates the flagship auto dealership that gave it its name. Several service floors below grade include retail space and a health club. The structure forms two courtyards at the base level with a sunbathed pool garden to the south, and a shaded activities court to the north. While interviewing Norten in 2015, the architect told me: "I believe,

one thing everyone is doing now is reinventing Modernism in his or her own way. I like to look at Modernism with the belief and conviction that it still has not given everything. And then, of course, the issues of natural environment, urban environment, social inclusion... we should continue looking for new possibilities, new responsibilities, and new opportunities within the realm of Modernism. These are all our common interests. I believe that romantic time of heroic manifestos doesn't exist anymore."

Juilliard School

Hypar Pavilion at Lincoln Center — Saddle

7

Hypar Pavilion at Lincoln Center — Saddle

069 D

10 Lincoln Center Plaza,
Lincoln Center
Diller Scofidio + Renfro
with FXFOWLE Architects
2010

1 to 66 Street-Lincoln Center

Sited on the edge of Hearst Plaza and 65th Street, the Hypar Pavilion is a new freestanding structure at Lincoln Center for the Performing Arts, that houses a restaurant topped by a public lawn.

Its dual character is achieved by a single architectural gesture in the shape of a saddle or a twisting parabolic roof. It is accessed at its single point of contact with Hearst Plaza. Climbing to the top of the saddle offers one the pure joy of encountering a patch of bucolic landscape that seems as if it just landed here from the countryside. Elizabeth Diller comments, "Hypar Pavilion's moment of invention came when we discovered how to design a destination restaurant without consuming public space on the Lincoln Center campus. The roof became a new kind of interface between public

and private, with an occupiable, twisting grass canopy over a glass pavilion restaurant." Hypar Pavilion continues Diller Scofidio + Renfro's strategic updates to the Lincoln Center campus, which include the redesign of Alice Tully Hall, the expansion and renovation of The Juilliard School, the public promenade project along the 65th Street, as well as plazas, sidewalks, stairs, and canopies. In my 2016 interview with Liz Diller and Ric Scofidio at their busy New York studio, Diller said: "The speed of change is now faster than it has ever been. Everything is being rethought; technology is changing our lives in every way. Yet, architecture hasn't really kept up with these changes. So, in our projects we critique architecture's relevance to the world that it is a part of. That's why so many conventions of our discipline have to be shaken up. The idea of nature is fascinating. The belief that something is natural is such an old-fashioned idea. It doesn't really exist anymore. Is anything natural? What can be stranger than to grow grass and trees on buildings? And look how this strange urban nature is perfectly accepted now. Where do you draw the line between what is constructed and what is natural?"

7

Photo: Iwan Baan

Alice Tully Hall and Juilliard School — Shark's Mouth

070 D

1941 Broadway, Lincoln Center
Diller Scofidio + Renfro
with FXFOWLE Architects
2009

🚇 to 66 Street-Lincoln Center

This dual-program project, like the Hypar Pavilion, also designed by New York-based Diller Scofidio + Renfro (DS+R), is the 2009 renovation and expansion of Pietro Belluschi's Brutalist original 1969 building, a concert hall at Lincoln Center for the Performing Arts. The project's scope includes the Juilliard School's grand entrance lobby, whose steps morph into seats for hanging out. The school's upper three floors are extruded out to the sidewalk toward Broadway, partly covering an existing triangular plaza. The cantilevered volume, with its tilted underside, serves as the framing canopy for the Alice Tully Hall expansion below. Its freestanding triangular amphitheater marks the building's corner where Broadway intersects with 65th Street, and evokes a shark's open mouth, with concrete steps looking like sharp teeth on its lower jaw. Despite this dramatic image, the newly glazed, triple-height, cable-net glass curtain wall enclosing an entrance lobby, box office, and café, projects an inviting see-through atmosphere, effectively merging interiors with the street. A large dance rehearsal studio hangs right in the shark's mouth, split into two unequal parts by the glass facade. Other major features include the Alice Tully Hall auditorium's interiors, a black box theater, an orchestra

rehearsal space, recording studio, jazz studios, a library expansion, an archive for rare music manuscripts, classrooms, and administrative offices. Of particular interest is the auditorium skin, which consists almost entirely of custom, backlit translucent wood veneer-and-resin panels that DS+R developed with building materials manufacturer 3form, specifically for the project. Panels can be peeled out to form gill-like acoustic baffles along the side-walls. Sections of the balcony and sidewalls give off a soft pinkish backlight as LEDs hidden behind them are illuminated. The architects call their lighting scheme "the blush." These blushing walls signal the start of performance.

In my 2016 interview with Ric Scofidio and Liz Diller, Scofidio said: "Aiming to simply solve problems means you already know what they are. That's why we try to be very critical of all the issues at hand and explore how architecture can define them. Every time we are handed a program we tear it apart and we continuously ask new questions. Nothing is fixed. We like to explore new territories. This means that some things get resolved properly and some things remain questionable. This produces a richer vocabulary for architecture. We get passionate about ideas and then try to find solutions that sometimes lead to inventing new technologies and programs."

7

Sketch by James Polshek

Photo: V. Belogolovsky

Photo: Frederick Phineas and Sandra Priest

**Rose Center for Earth and
Space at the American
Museum of Natural History —
Globus**
75–208 79th Street, Upper West Side
Polshek Partnership (now Ennead)
2000

071 D

B C
to 81 Street-Museum of Natural History
1 to 79 Street

Designed by James Polshek and his New York-based firm, which is now called Ennead, the Rose Center includes a new entrance to the American Museum of Natural History. It is located on the northern side of the museum complex, and faces 81st Street. Its most breathtaking feature is a six-story-high glass cube that contains an 87-foot (27-meter)-diameter illuminated sphere with two theaters within it, called the "Hayden Planetarium" or the "Hayden Sphere." Slightly angled columns support it in such a way that it appears to float. Polshek has referred to this project as a "cosmic cathedral." The bold, platonic-solid geometry of the complex is a striking contrast both to the museum's original neo-Romanesque building and its historical neighborhood, which remains largely undisturbed by contemporary architecture. When finished in 2000, the structure was one of the first signs that a new kind of architecture, unafraid to celebrate late-20th-century materials and technologies, had arrived in New York. Now the museum is involved in another experimental project, commissioning Chicago-based architect Jeanne Gang of Studio Gang. She is working to realize a grand, 21st-century-worthy addition on the west side of the museum that will face Columbus Avenue.

7

Photo: V. Belogolovsky

Manhattan: Upper Manhattan

Morningside Heights, Hamilton Heights,
Washington Heights, Inwood

8

074 Barnard College, The Diana Center

073 Northwest Corner Building

Lerner Hall Student Center — Catwalk

072 C

2920 Broadway near 115th
Street at Columbia University
campus, Morningside Heights
*Bernard Tschumi with
Gruzen Samton Architects*
1999

🚇 to 116 Street-Columbia University

Bernard Tschumi, the Swiss-born, New York- and Paris-based architect, designed Lerner Hall Student Center while he was serving as the Dean of Columbia University School of Architecture. Visually, it is three different buildings in one — it is two solid rectangular blocks that bookend a glazed, four-story volume in the middle. The student hub brings together a range of social spaces and organizations previously scattered across campus. These range from student clubs, restaurants, party and exhibition spaces, rehearsal halls, and conference rooms to a theater, cinema, radio station, and dining hall. Finally, there is a large campus bookstore buried in the basement. The building's east and west wings don't pretend to be anything but contextual, simply borrowing their brick and granite facades from both the Beaux-Arts architecture of McKim, Mead & White's 1894 campus master plan, and the neighborhood's residential buildings lined up along Broadway. The building's middle link has a personality of its own, animated and defined by the movement of students and visitors along a set of criss-crossing glass-floored ramps that are appropriately fashioned into a series of catwalks. Their gentle slopes, dramatically lit at night, put on an unapologetic display behind a full-height glass curtain wall, much like a billboard. The hub's cinematic facade literally transmits various internal activities to the campus. On occasion the ramps have served as a multi-story stage for dance performances and fashion shows. Note the intricately futuristic steel and glass components articulated in a machine-like, high-tech architecture that brings a strong contrast to this still predominantly stone- and brick-clad part of the city. In our 2004 interview, I asked Tschumi to reflect on the criticism of some Columbia University students whose opinion is that Lerner Hall's glass atrium is not functional. The architect responded: "It is not meant to be functional. It is meant to be social. Look at the grand steps in front of the Low Library. It is not functional either, right? But it is used as a gathering center of the community. The Student Center and its ramps are places where you can see everything from everywhere. It is a very large building and it is a vertical building. So as an architect, I asked myself — how do you establish a vertical community? How do you establish a vertical connection? And I think that part works very well!"

Photos: Courtesy of Bernard Tschumi Architects

Northwest Corner Building — Gameboard

073 C

550 West 120th Street,
Morningside Heights
*Rafael Moneo with Moneo
Brock Studio*
2010

🌐 to 116 Street-Columbia University

As its name suggests, the Northwest Corner Building is situated at the northwest corner of Columbia University's historic Morningside Heights Campus, where Broadway meets 120th Street. This quiet but tough structure is the only design by Madrid-based architect Rafael Moneo to be realized in New York. Moneo is a master at creating strong modern buildings that engage in appropriate, yet tense dialogs with their historical contexts. The building in question fits in well on this site, while responding to a number of complex issues that only truly modern building could address. The 14-story structure, which is considerably higher than its neighbors, forms a new gateway to the campus by negotiating a 35-foot (10.5-meter) split between the street and the campus through a series of publicly accessible stairs, escalators, and a popular, spacious café. This interdisciplinary science building features a research library, auditorium, laboratories, classrooms, offices, and study spaces, in addition to housing a basketball and volleyball gymnasium. From an architectural point of view, the building's fragmented facade, with its taut steel-and-aluminum framed grid, filled in with diagonal, ribbed aluminum fins and louvers, is arranged into a seemingly random but lively pattern that evokes a gameboard as large as the building itself. The directions of fins and louvers express the uneven loads and stresses on the building, which is supported by an enormous truss that spans the gym below. The building's campus-side facade is largely dressed in glass. The street-level lobby, clad in richly veined Portuguese marble, is also of interest.

8

Photo: Michael Moran

Barnard College,
The Diana
Center — Cascade
3009 Broadway between
116th and 120th Streets,
Morningside Heights
Marion Weiss and Michael Manfredi
of Weiss/Manfredi
2010

074 **C**

① to 116 Street-Columbia University

The Diana Center is an innovative nexus for artistic, social, and intellectual life at Barnard College, a private women's liberal arts school founded in 1889 because in those days Columbia University did not admit women. Now the Diana Center is attended both by female and male students. Its new building faces the Lehman Lawn, the core of the tight campus located on a large block along Broadway between 116th and 120th Streets.

The campus is made up of noble Beaux-Arts buildings, predominately dressed in red brick and terracotta. The new structure, designed by Marion Weiss and Michael Manfredi, founding partners of New York-based Weiss/Manfredi, brings together previously dispersed programs, including art, architecture, theater, and art history, as well as faculty offices, a dining room, a café, a 100-seat black box theater, a 500-seat multipurpose event space, and a green roof. The new building is defined by a diagonal alignment of several ascending double-height atria that cascade toward the north end, along the building's Broadway side, a visual extension of Lehman Lawn, and also by a series of glazed stairs and platforms projecting over the campus side. The terraces provide a vital mix of study spaces and bring natural light and continuous views into the mixed-use seven-story structure, an effective vertical campus that

encourages interaction and interdisciplinary collaboration. The Diana Center's facades consist of a luminous, energy-efficient curtain wall of fritted glass panels of varying widths and degrees of transparency, opacity, and gradients of terra-cotta color. Both the arrangement of the stepped atria and fussiness of the building's facades contribute to our perceiving its Broadway side as a beautiful cascade. This adventurous building is open to the public.

Photos: Albert Večerka/Esto

City College Spitzer School of Architecture — Piranesi

075 C

141 Convent Avenue and
W 135th St, Hamilton Heights
Rafael Viñoly
2009

❷ ❸ to 135 Street

The new Spitzer Architecture School building at City College was designed by Rafael Viñoly, the Uruguayan-born, New York-based architect. It is the first new academic building on the upper Manhattan campus of the City University of New York since 1982. The new building is a thorough renovation of an existing reinforced-concrete structure — a five-story, Modernist building designed and constructed as a library in the late 1950s. Viñoly cut a large square opening in the center to create the floor-to-roof atrium, a Piranesian space that is crisscrossed by multiple steel stairs and bridges under a skylight. The shaft is not simply to provide circulation shortcuts through the building, but to establish connectivity and sight lines between floors and promote interactivity and spontaneous encounters among students and faculty. The building is clad in precast concrete with deep, framed openings subdivided by aluminum sun-shading louvers. It is accessed via two flights of stairs running next to a retaining wall holding a diagonally raised lawn with a small entry plaza. Once inside, the ground floor gallery, which occupies the base of the central atrium just a few steps away from the entrance, immediately pulls you in with its open circulation through and around, and the spatially intriguing views overhead. The interiors feature an architecture library, open-plan design studios, faculty offices, and double-height informal lounge areas around the open atrium for socializing and pin-up presentations. Weather permitting, an open-air amphitheater, painted yellow and sitting directly over the central skylight with a full-height clerestory on three sides, provides additional classroom space on the roof with unobstructed views over the Manhattan skyline. In our 2007 interview, Viñoly said: "The first thing that makes a good building is a challenge of a building type, which is transformative. I do believe in evolution. If you did a house one way, there must be another way of doing it better. Architecture, at the end of the day, is a compositional business. It is like jazz. If you ever played jazz, it is incredibly free, but it has much more rigidity than people tend to realize. By rigidity, I mean it has structure. It has moments of freedom. But you need to have some form of cohesive composition behind it."

Photos: Courtesy of Rafael Viñoly Architects

Sugar Hill Development —
Shift
400 West 155th Street,
Washington Heights
*David Adjaye of
Adjaye Associates with
SLCE Architects*
2014

B D to 155 Street

076 C

Designed by British-Ghanaian architect
David Adjaye of Adjaye Associates, the
Sugar Hill Development, in the historical
Sugar Hill district of Harlem, is a mixed-
use complex that offers a new typology,
both visually and programmatically. The
building brings together affordable housing, including transitional apartments for
the homeless; a preschool (an early child-
hood education center), and the Sugar Hill

Photo: Ed Reeve

Children's Museum of Art & Storytelling. It also houses the offices for Broadway Housing Communities (BHC), a community-based nonprofit that fights homelessness and inequality in Washington Heights and West Harlem. Despite being built on a tight budget the building challenges the traditional New York model for affordable public housing blocks commonly referred to as "projects." Projects are cookie-cutter buildings, many dating to the 1950s, that not only lack character because of the limited arsenal of design scenarios, but also were made of poor-quality materials and not well maintained; they transmit the fact that their occupants are poor. The 13-story edifice rises on sloping 155th Street. It steps back at the 9th floor, where the BHC offices are located, to minimize the building's impact on the street and leave space for 10-foot (3-meter)-wide set-back terraces on one side and a cantilever on the other. This move produces a characteristic shift, the most apparent feature when the building is encountered from its narrow side facades. The building's front and back facades are further fractured into multiple stepped planes that address the scale of Gothic revival rowhouses in the area. The facades are clad in tinted, textured, precast concrete panels that are punched by slightly misaligned windows of various sizes. These panels sparkle,

with sunlight adding a shimmery effect throughout the day. In our 2008 interview at Adjaye's London studio, the architect told me: "I am a planetary architect, and as other architects, I work by tracking economies and places where the patrons are. They provide opportunities for work. My interest in architecture is to find ways of seeing each other and new ways of being with each other. I see architecture as an agency to facilitate these kinds of opportunities within public life. For me, architecture depicts how we write the story of our civilization."

8

**Columbia University
Medical Center — Sculpture**
104 Haven Avenue between
West 171st and 172nd Streets,
Washington Heights
Diller Scofidio + Renfro with Gensler
2016

077 **B**

Ⓐ to 175 Street

The Vagelos Education Center is a whimsical sculpture-like 14-story structure on Columbia University's upper Manhattan medical campus near the George Washington Bridge. While the building's north side is as conventional-looking as anything that surrounds it, the building's visually stunning south side is a teetering stack of cantilevered terraces, indoor bleacher seats, lounges, and stairs. The architects call this array of explosively active parts clad in white, orange, and Douglas fir panels stained a burnt sienna a "study cascade." In my 2018 interview with Charles Renfro, the architect explained this wildly articulated building's

8

design intention: "The project was built on a site that was far too small to fit all the programs. So, it was clear that we had to make a vertical building. Then we separated all the classrooms and lecture halls vertically. The cascade of auditoria is what makes all the social life and it is also what makes the image of the building. The classrooms are simply stacked up in the back; they are anonymous from the outside. We wanted this building to have an image. All of our projects have strong images from a pedagogical desire to educate about each building. The image of the building is a description of what is happening inside; it was not driven by wanting to make a particular image or facade. The result is a transmission of the building's internal guts. And that's what makes the overall image. We try to display the mission of the building as the image. Guts, meaning not the infrastructure like in the Centre Pompidou, but like interconnected organs. It looks a bit like a sculpture by German-French abstract artist Jean Arp."

Campbell Sports Center — Index Finger

078 B

West 218th Street and
Broadway, Inwood
Steven Holl Architects
2013

1 to 215 Street

Located on West 218th Street near Broadway, at the very tip of Manhattan, the Campbell Sports Center forms a new gateway to the Baker Athletics Complex, the primary athletics facility for Columbia University's outdoor sports program. This unusual structure can be described in many ways but it is not a typical building that sits like an object on the ground. Despite the fact that fundamental elements of architecture are all here — columns, external terraces and stairs, handrails, parapets, windows, as well as flat and straight roofs and facades wrapped in reflective, metallic panels — the overall impression is anything but familiar. The entire assemblage is completely reimagined and rethought like

a half-solved puzzle. The resulting composition feels awkward, intriguing, and as intense as the postures of athletes being trained within. Yet, the apparatus-like structure seems quite at home when seen under and through the elevated tracks of the 1 subway line hovering over Broadway or against the background of skeletal towers of the Broadway Bridge over the Harlem River just a couple of blocks to the north. In the words of its designer, New York-based architect Steven Holl, who grew up in Washington State, the center's purpose is: "Serving the mind, the body, and the mind/body for aspiring scholar-athletes." The design concept is "points on the ground, lines in space" — like the diagrams coaches use to explain plays in football, soccer, and baseball — developed from point foundations on the sloping site. The presence of numerous exterior stairs also evokes the classic Chutes and Ladders board game, while, when seen from above, the upper floor recalls a giant index finger. In our 2004 conversation, Holl said: "There is a need for theory and philosophy in everything in life. I agree with old philosophers who said that an unexamined life is not worth living. We should think about every little thing we do, including energy saving, global warming, and politics. I think one of the greatest tragedies of our time is that there is not enough theory and philosophy. There is not enough truly deep thinking and discussion about things that we go out in the world and do thoughtlessly. Architecture, for sure, needs theory and philosophy because it is a more permanent art."

MAS COBERTURA 4G LTE

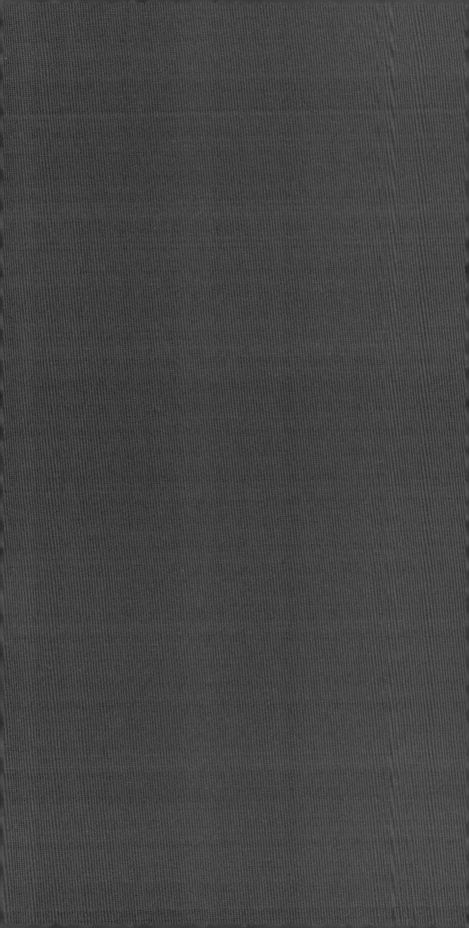

Brooklyn

DUMBO, Brooklyn Navy Yard, Downtown Brooklyn, Fort Greene, Prospect Heights, Crown Heights, Clinton Hill, Greenpoint, East Williamsburg, Coney Island

9

086 Brooklyn Children's Museum

Jane's Carousel Pavilion — Music Box

Brooklyn Bridge Park, DUMBO
Jean Nouvel
2011

🅐 🅒 to High Street
❷ ❸ to Clark Street
🅕 to York Street

By itself, the clear pavilion that houses Jane's Carousel can hardly be considered architecture, let alone iconic, which brings up the critical question of whether architecture can be separated from its site, content, and the story of its creation? Can it be discussed and critiqued one part at a time? Not in this case. Many elements comprise its totality: the project's enclosure and the fantastic site in Brooklyn Bridge Park, the historical carousel and the history of its glory days, rescue, and restoration, and finally, the fact that the project was designed by Paris-based architect Jean Nouvel. All of these factors make this work invaluable and instantly both a historical landmark and icon of contemporary architecture. And not only does this smallish piece of architecture look like a music box, it sounds like one. The wooden, 48-horse,

two-chariot carousel, originally known as the Idora Park Merry-Go-Round, was built by Philadelphia Toboggan Company in 1922. It became the first carousel listed on the National Register of Historic Places in 1975. David Walentas purchased the carousel in 1984 from Idora Park, an amusement park in Youngstown, Ohio, after the park closed. Walentas is a self-made billionaire who founded Two Trees Management company and most notably made a fortune rebuilding DUMBO, where he lives. Walentas' wife Jane, an artist, oversaw a painstaking 27-year, $15 million restoration, and personally scraped a dozen or so layers of paint off the carousel and its horses to reach their original state. The restored carousel found its home within Nouvel's display case in the shadow of the Brooklyn Bridge in 2011. Interestingly, David was looking for an iconic catalyst piece with history, specifically, a carousel, to be placed at the waterfront, as a part of his then-just-being-imagined DUMBO redevelopment. So, when the Idora Park Carousel was put up for sale, Jane was already in search of one. The square-tube steel-framed, 4-inch (10-cm)-thick acrylic enclosure can be opened on two sides — north and south — to provide a more open-air experience.

Photos: Roland Halbe

At night, white shades can be drawn so one can see the shadows of wooden horses dancing around the walls. Still, a bigger question remains — why one of the greatest and busiest architects alive was commissioned to do such a small-scale project? Back in 1999, David Walentas commissioned Nouvel for another project, a nine-story, 250-room pier-like hotel that was to cantilever 134 feet (41 meters) out over the East River. That quixotic project surely would have been iconic and was perhaps ahead of its time, and it

(literally) never got off the ground. But when the time came to enclose the newly restored Jane's Carousel, Nouvel was the architect Jane wished to do the work because he was known to do magic with buildings made of glass and pure air. Initially, he could not understand why a carousel would need an enclosure, since in Paris and most other places around the world, carousels operate in warm weather and then are packed away during winters. Not here in New York, where they spin, spin, and spin.

Image: Courtesy of S9 Architecture

Dock 72 — Caterpillar
63 Flushing Ave #300,
Brooklyn Navy Yard
S9 Architecture
2019

080 A

F to York Street
East River Ferry to South Williamsburg

Located on the waterfront in the heart of Brooklyn Navy Yard, Dock 72, a 16-story building, will be home to creative and tech firms, most notably WeWork, a global network of workspaces. The company collaborated on the building's program development and will occupy a third of its total area. The building was planned and designed to encourage innovation and collaboration between occupants. It will house workspaces, a specialty food hall, a health and wellness center, a conference center, multiple lounges for socializing and meetings, a lawn with games, bike valet parking, and an outdoor basketball court. Designed by S9 Architecture, the building is inspired by the formal language of the ships once built on the site. The entire building is propped up on 20 sets of 42-foot (13-meter)-tall V-shaped columns to protect it from potential flood damage in the event of a superstorm. It is these "legs" that give the building a likeness of a caterpillar in motion. Tours can be booked on the Brooklyn Navy Yard website.

9 DeKalb Avenue — Minaret
9 DeKalb Avenue,
Downtown Brooklyn
SHoP Architects
2020

081 A

2 **3** to Hoyt Street
B **Q** **R** to DeKalb Avenue

The new residential tower, 9 DeKalb Avenue, designed by New York-based SHoP Architects will become the first supertall building in Brooklyn, reaching the height of 1,066 feet (325 meters). It will join other recently built high-rises in the area. The 500-apartment building is being developed by JDS Development Group, a local real estate development company that performs all of the construction on its own projects. The firm has teamed up with SHoP Architects on many projects. The tower's design is not rooted in SHoP's desire to transform the skyline alone. Rising right next to the compact, neoclassical Brooklyn Dime Savings Bank, a landmarked building that will be integrated into the new residential complex, 9 DeKalb will take over much of the small triangular block defined by DeKalb Avenue, Fulton Avenue, and Fleet Street. The new 73-story tower that incorporates multiple setbacks evokes a minaret, due to both its extreme slenderness and its close proximity to the bank's neoclassical dome, which in this new setting recalls a mosque typology. At street level the tower will create a series of new pathways and public spaces. The bank's historic interior will be restored and repurposed to form part of a new mid-block connection for pedestrians between Flatbush Avenue and nearby Fulton Street, densely dotted with shops and restaurants. The new building will be accented with a palette of materials, ranging from marble to bronze, to evoke the rich City Beautiful detailing of the bank. The tower's plan is formed from interlocking hexagons, referencing the original geometry of the bank and optimizing the constraints of this tight site. In 2013, when I interviewed SHoP's partner Gregg Pasquarelli he talked about his firm's business model: "Architects, who are great creative thinkers, should be generalists and not only specialists. They should start getting involved with their projects on a variety of levels — understand the finance and invest money, get involved in politics, control the construction process, envision ideas for how their buildings will be maintained and used in the future. They can't just be designers. For us to grab back these territories can only be done through the use of emerging technologies, and that is exactly what is happening. The more engaged and integrated into the building process we get, the more valuable our contribution will be to the built environment overall."

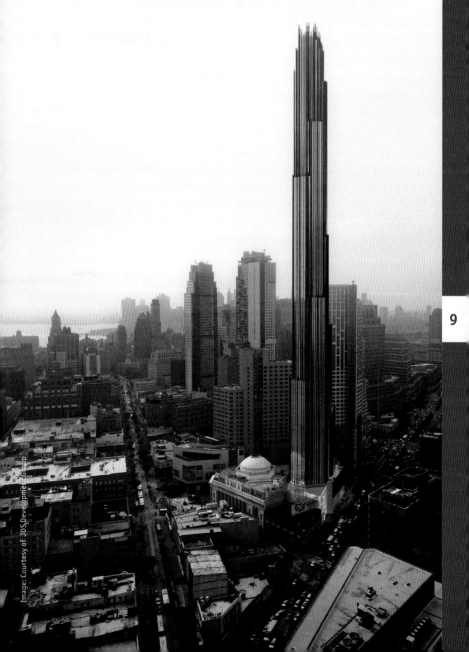

9

BAM South — Tetris Facade

300 Ashland Place near
Flatbush Avenue, Fort Greene
Enrique Norten of Ten Arquitectos
2016

Ⓑ Ⓓ Ⓝ Ⓠ Ⓡ ② ③ ④ ⑤
to Atlantic Avenue-Barclays Center

The New York-based Mexican architect Enrique Norten of Ten Arquitectos designed the new mixed-use BAM South building. It marks the gateway to the Brooklyn Academy of Music, a center for progressive and avant-garde performing arts. Norten also won the 2002 international competition to design the Brooklyn Visual and Performing Arts Library at this same site, the triangle defined by Flatbush, Ashland, and Lafayette Avenues. The architect envisioned that unbuilt library as a bold, captivating structure in the form of a prow of a glass ship. That project did not obtain funding, but Norten's vision for a vibrant cultural hub and newly energized streetscape is now realized with the much grander BAM South project. The 32-story tower with its slim footprint occupies the south portion of the site and leaves most of it to a new public plaza. The building's base is a series of landscaped terraces that create an active, urban experience and screen traffic noise and pollution along Flatbush. Several of the tower's lower floors are reserved for cultural tenants that include the performing arts organization 651 Arts, Brooklyn Academy of Music cinemas, and a new branch of the Brooklyn Public Library. The tower also houses retail space and rental apartments. The building's extensive east and west facades are clad in a skin of continuous folded light gray metal panels punched by windows and air-conditioning-unit grilles that look like a giant Tetris pattern. In our 2015 interview, Norten said: "Architecture has become a destination. But I don't think the weirdest is the best. I don't think you need to do the strangest thing, the most unexpected thing in order to do good architecture. Is that a good question to ask — how can I do something that had never been done before? I think a number of very intelligent architects are falling into this trap of constantly trying to overdo what they have done before and what others have done. Where does that lead and where does that end? Architecture is not a competition of strange objects."

Photo: Alan Karchmer

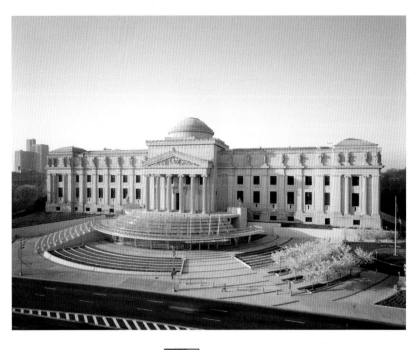

Brooklyn Museum Entry Pavilion and Plaza — Peacock

083 A

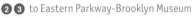

200 Eastern Parkway,
Prospect Heights
Polshek Partnership (now Ennead)
2004

② ③ to Eastern Parkway-Brooklyn Museum
Ⓑ Ⓠ to Prospect Park

This futuristic steel and glass entrance pavilion, which resembles a peacock's tail, is the new point of access to the McKim, Mead & White-designed Beaux-Arts Brooklyn Museum dating from 1897.

Photos: Courtesy of Brooklyn Museum

The hemispherical stepped-roof structure, designed by James Stewart Polshek of New York-based Ennead, was built in an area once occupied by a monumental staircase that headed off the formal, colonnaded entrance portico. Ever since the stair's removal in 1939, this side of the building had looked unfinished. Opened in 2004, the new entrance transformed and energized the Museum's identity on Eastern Parkway. In front of it is a semicircular plaza of concentric arcs radiating outward from the portico, with uneven segments of grass beds, benches, a stepped seating area, and a delightfully dancing computer-programmed fountain by California-based WET Design. What now is the front of the imposing Greco-Roman building was once planned as a minor facade on the side of a never-completed, colossal complex that would have been the largest single museum structure in the world. Less than a quarter of that grand scheme was ever realized. Today the complex feels like a truly modern building that rejects any nostalgic attitude. It is open-ended and forward-looking, which is a good thing because there are still many circulation issues that will need to be addressed in future alterations. The Polshek design is exemplary in the way it treats the mother building as a working model and not as an untouchable relic.

9

Barclays Center — Whale
620 Atlantic Avenue,
Fort Greene
SHoP Architects with Ellerbe Becket (now part of AECOM)
2012

084 A

B D N Q R 2 3 4 5
to Atlantic Avenue-Barclays Center

The Barclays Center, an indoor arena with capacity for 19,000 spectators, is located at one of the busiest urban intersections in the city, Flatbush and Atlantic Avenues. Apart from hosting concerts and other entertainment events, it is home to the NBA's Brooklyn Nets and NHL's New York Islanders. The arena and the Brooklyn Nets are owned by Russian billionaire Mikhail Prokhorov. The London-based banking group Barclays agreed to pay the Nets $400 million over a period of 20 years for the naming rights. The building's fluid form, clad in rusty steel panels, evokes a monumental whale leaping out of water for a breath of fresh air. Despite being a freestanding building, this ambitious structure is, it would be fair to say, skin deep; there is absolutely no relation between the wrapper and the unremarkable interiors by sports-facilities specialist Ellerbe Becket. But what a skin it is! The Center's facade is made up of 12,000 metal panels, each of which is unique.

This was achieved through the firm's mastery of the latest parametric technology and thorough control of design, fabrication, and assembly processes. While interviewing SHoP's partner Gregg Pasquarelli in 2013, the architect explained to me the intentions behind this fantastic project: "For us, the Barclays Center is a performance-based building. This is an enormous building in a neighborhood of 19th-century houses. The idea was to divide the building horizontally, making these swoops of solid and transparent bends... A major concern was to develop the facades, to play with the texture and scale, to work with the surrounding buildings. We chose rusted-looking weathered-steel because we wanted a radically modern building — and yet a building that would fit both with the industrial character and neighboring brownstones of that part of Brooklyn. The skin is multilayered and porous, which is achieved with variably spaced steel panels in different shapes and backlighting. So, day and night the perception of the building is constantly changing. Starting with the research about 15 years ago" — he continued — "we already knew that the computer does not care if the pieces it needs to fabricate are the same or all different. So, if we can manage the control of such versatile systems by thinking through how everything

is going to be built and assembled, you can make anything you can dream of. Now, mass customization, where everything is unique, becomes possible. In the case of the Barclays Center facades, the smaller parts were assembled at the factory, came to the site as bigger panels, and were simply clipped to the building exactly the same way as if they were all the same. I don't think that the complex curvatures that are achieved in this project could have been built even five years ago. The technology was not there yet. Now we can do it." The arena is a part of a scaled down version of the original Frank Gehry-designed controversial 22-acre (9-hectare) multi-billion-dollar Atlantic Yards redevelopment plan that also included 16 residential towers. It was scrapped as too costly. The current project will include three modular high-rise residential buildings along the southern and eastern elevations of the arena site fronting Dean Street, Flatbush Avenue, and 6th Avenue. All towers are designed by SHoP; two of the three buildings are already built. Together they will contain about 1,500 apartments. Reaching 32 stories, one of the towers will be the tallest modular building in the world.

9

Photos: Bruce Damonte

**Brooklyn Botanic Garden
Visitor Center — Serpentine**
990 Washington Avenue,
Crown Heights
*Marion Weiss and Michael
Manfredi of Weiss/Manfredi*
2012

085 A

❷❸
to Eastern Parkway-Brooklyn Museum
Ⓑ Ⓠ to Prospect Park

The city of New York has zoos and botanical gardens in every borough. New pavilions and the remodeling of old ones offer architects unique opportunities for innovation. Yet, just one such recent structure was selected for this guide, the Brooklyn Botanic Garden Visitor Center designed by New York duo Marion Weiss and Michael Manfredi of Weiss/Manfredi. The new formal entrance into the garden is situated on a small plaza next to the Brooklyn Museum. It is constructed as a "natural" environment and is comprised of two sinuous pavilions that gradually transition from architectural forms facing the street into a structured landscape that merges with the botanic garden. The pavilions house an information lobby, orientation room, spaces for events and exhibitions, gift shop, and a café. A ribbon of shaded breezeway separates the two pavilions. More than anything, the Visitor Center provokes curiosity and interest in the garden's extensive collection:

It is a legible point of arrival and orientation, an interface between garden and city, culture, and cultivation. The building is conceived as inhabitable topography that defines a new threshold between the city and the constructed landscapes of one of the most beautiful urban gardens in the world. The Center's serpentine form is generated by the garden's existing pathways and is defined by its undulating landscaped roof, a series of landscaped terraces, and curved fritted glass walls. The structure is never seen in its entirety, and looking at it, one never quite sees where the building ends and the landscape begins.

9

Brooklyn Children's Museum — Toy

145 Brooklyn Avenue,
Crown Heights
Rafael Viñoly of Viñoly Architects
2008

086 A

Ⓐ Ⓒ to Nostrand Avenue
❸ to Kingston Avenue

The intersection of St. Marks and Brooklyn Avenues in Crown Heights cannot fail to make an impression on any passerby, particularly a kid. Look up, behind the leafy three branches, and you will see a toy-like yellow submarine gliding and turning the corner. This curious apparatus, wrapped in yellow ceramic tile and equipped with portholes at various levels, is propped up by red, green, and gray oversized building blocks that hold it afloat over unassuming Brooklyn residential streets lined with turn-of-the-century stately brownstones and multistory brick coops with their top floors stylized into an array of pitched roofs. Designed by New York architect Rafael Viñoly, this unconventional 2008 structure is a popular Brooklyn Children's Museum. Founded in 1899 as the first children's museum in the U.S., it was originally based in a house at the corner of Brooklyn Avenue and Prospect Place. It was not until 1977 that the Museum moved to its current address. The Viñoly addition doubled the existing structure in size by building on top of what was largely tacked under the adjacent Brower Park. The original low-profile building was designed by late New York architect Hugh

Hardy (1932–2017) of Hardy Holzman Pfeiffer. The honking, sculptural form of the new museum serves as a new beacon in the neighborhood, which is not known for distinctive architecture. The Viñoly building that adds a library, exhibition galleries, café, and classrooms, follows a basic L-shaped plan of a two-story dynamic mass around the existing rooftop terrace and outdoor theater. Since 2015, the roof terrace has hosted a creature-like pavilion made of translucent high-tech fabric stretched over a framework of tubular steel. It was designed by New York-based Japanese architect Toshiko Mori. While discussing Viñoly's design process in our 2007 interview, the architect said: "I work on design problems through large-scale study models. This is something that I learned from Cesar Pelli, and that Pelli and Saarinen learned from Louis Kahn. That is a fantastic tool. And that is something that makes a designer an architect. I don't believe in sitting down with brilliant people who tell me something and I am then supposed to come up with something that fits their parameters. I draw it, and then I work it out in models."

Photos: Michael Moran

Pratt Institute Higgins Hall — Lantern

087 A

61 St. James Place near Lafayette Avenue, Clinton Hill
Steven Holl with Rogers Marvel Architects
2005

C G to Clinton-Washington Avenues

Photo: V. Belogolovsky

The new Higgins Hall is an inserted, missing-link structure that bridges the gap between two late-19th-century buildings. Following the 1996 fire that destroyed much of the Architecture School that occupies this part of the Pratt Institute's campus, the three-story building, designed by Steven Holl was completed in 2005. The floor plates of the surviving north and south wings don't align, and the architect calls the space between the misaligned buildings a "dissonant zone." It now marks the new entry to the school and serves primarily as a social connector space, distinguished by a glass facade that is both clear and translucent and made up of double-glazed textured channel-glass panels that glow as a lantern at night. It is animated day and night by the shadowy figures of people moving within. New courtyards facing east and west are paved in red brick salvaged from the burned structure. The east-facing court overlooks the green yards of the inner block, while the west court serves as the main entrance on St. James Place. Apart from being the main entry to the school, the new structure houses a lobby, sunken event space, exhibition gallery, a large auditorium, digital resource center, review room, studios, and workshops. The dissonance between the floor plates is accentuated by a system of open connecting ramps bathed in sunlight coming from both facades and a two-throated skylight from the top. Holl told me in our 2004 interview: "Architecture is a link between ideas and tensions, philosophies and hopes, and the materiality of the world, the light and the space. Architecture embodies all of that. Architects spend their time and energy on the design. It is the space and forms that radiate it back, and people can feel it." Arrange your visit inside the school ahead of time, as the entrance is guarded and not open to the public. For guided tours contact the school's Admissions Office on the second floor of Myrtle Hall at 200 Willoughby Avenue.

Watercolor by Steven Holl

Newtown Creek Wastewater Treatment Plant — Eggs

327 Greenpoint Ave, Greenpoint
Polshek Partnership
(now Ennead Architects)
2010

Ⓖ to Greenpoint Avenue

Located in Brooklyn's Greenpoint neighborhood, the Newtown Creek Wastewater Treatment Plant is the largest of New York City's 14 wastewater treatment facilities. It is situated on 53 acres (21.5 hectares) and serves more than one million people in parts of Brooklyn, Queens, and Manhattan. Polshek Partnership, now known as Ennead Architects, oversaw its master plan, which included both a renovation and an extensive new design. The plant's most pronounced feature is its group of eight futuristic, stainless-steel-clad digester eggs that play a critical role in processing sludge. Reaching the height of 140 feet (42 meters) and being dramatically illuminated in blue at night, they stand as a symbol of civic service, as they are highly visible from nearby busy highways and bridges in Brooklyn and Queens against the backdrop of Manhattan's skyscrapers. When some Greenpoint residents tried to resist the proposed expansion of the plant, the city worked with the community to include public amenities in the project plan as a part of the city's law decreeing that one percent of public works expenditures must be spent on art. As a result, the architects worked with three local artists on a series of art projects throughout the plant. Vito Acconci created the waterfall and watercourse features in and around the visitor center for education programs. Hervé Descottes designed the illumination, including the blue lighting of the digester eggs and the white lighting of the walkways. George Trakas designed the nature walk, which includes several sculptural elements. Tours of the Digester Eggs at the Newtown Creek Wastewater Treatment Plant are hosted three times a year: in February, April, and October.

Photo: Jeff Goldberg/Esto

Carroll House — Slant

2 Monitor Street, corner
of Richardson Street,
East Williamsburg
*Ada Tolla and Giuseppe Lignano
of LOT-EK*
2016

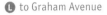 089 A

🄻 to Graham Avenue

Carroll House in East Williamsburg is the
work of New York-based architect couple
Ada Tolla and Giuseppe Lignano of LOT-EK.
Both were raised in Italy and educated at
Columbia University in New York. The project is no less than a revolution as far as
new approaches to single-family house
design in New York City are concerned.
Bluntly disregarding the predictable co-
lonial pastiche that has become a norm
in our city, the architects instead posed a
question that no one dared to pose before
them — what is a contemporary dwelling?
They used standard shipping containers
as building blocks to construct this house
on a typical corner lot for an adventurous
client who gave the architects a rare carte
blanche. In their experimental quest they
achieved a conceptually-driven form of a
house that has become a delightful space
to inhabit and to explore unconventional
ways of interacting between inside and
outside. The following excerpts are from
my 2017 meeting with the architects. Ada
Tolla: "To us, the shipping container is an
ongoing speculation and we always modify
it. We started from the generic container
stack that you see near ports and highways; we collected 21 containers to fit
the site and then we cut the whole stack

diagonally along both the top and bottom, creating a striking profile. The top cut
opens up containers, and every time the
diagonal meets the top of the container,
we close it with large glass doors to allow access to each deck, offering light and
cross ventilation at all levels. A steel stair
along the north wall connects all outdoor
spaces." Giuseppe Lignano: "Our lot is typical in New York; it is 25 feet [7.5 m] wide
and 100 feet [30 m] long. So, we used three
8-foot [2.5-m]-wide containers on the
short front and two 40-foot [12 m]-long
and one 20-foot [6-m]-long containers on
the long side. The key idea was to manip-
ulate a container stack and do something
monolithic and sculptural to create private
space on the inside and, at the same time,
open up the space to interesting possibilities. The use of the containers allowed us
to get away from the existing typology and
create a new one. For us the container is
a vehicle to invent new architecture."

9

West 8th Subway Station — Wave

West 8th Subway Station,
Coney Island
Vito Acconci
2006

090 A

🄵 🅀 to West 8 Street-NY Aquarium

Designed by Vito Acconci (1940–2017), the late artist, poet, architect, and the father of performance and video art, West 8th Subway Station, called *WAVE-A-WALL*, is a total work of art that envelops the elevated station's facade enclosure and connecting stairs. Inspired by a roaring ocean wave, walls turn into waves here and waves into walls. Undulating walls are sliced, peeled, and twisted to open the space up to natural light, while MTA-standard steel panels and woven mesh are morphed into sinuous ribbon windows, shelves, seats, canopies, and skylights. The artist commented on his design, saying: "The facade itself should be a wave, like a wave in the ocean, like a wave of sand. The facade waves out, and bulges out, to enclose the stairway up to the station. A ramp to the station: the facade waves up and down, it waves out, it breaks to make an entrance. The facade twists from in to out, and vice versa; when it reaches a breaking point, it opens to make a view. Here and there the facade bulges just far enough in or out to make a long seat." The inspiration for the striking and unique subway station's design comes from all around — the historic Coney Island Boardwalk, the Cyclone roller coaster, the New York Aquarium next door, the beach, and of course, the twisting and waving subway tracks. In our

2015 interview at the artist's Brooklyn studio, Acconci said: "I don't like the kind of art that only allows you to be in front of it. The idea of being in front of something, but not inside of it, is terrifying to me. The fluidity comes from me wanting to be in two different places at the same time. So, spaces and places start to flow. They merge. Not just spaces, but also programs. Rather than attract attention to something I have done, I want people to pay attention to what's around them." When I asked whether Acconci sees his West 8th Street Subway Station as an artwork the architect responded: "I don't think I see anything I do as art. It may be architecture that can be called art. Architecture is the opposite of an image. Architecture is about motion and experience. Architecture should not be straightforward. It should be intuitive and multifunctional." I came to this station to take a few pictures one sunny morning and could not leave for a good part of a whole hour. The space is full of discoveries and absolutely worth a long commute from Manhattan, especially since there is so much to do in this area if you come in warm weather. The space is magically cinematic and uplifting, so much so that the station's state of maintenance, which is appalling, dissipates from conciseness and becomes secondary.

Photos: V. Belogolovsky

Ocean Wonders: Sharks! at New York Aquarium — Swirls

091 A

602 Surf Avenue,
Coney Island
Portico Group and ESKW
2018

F Q to West 8 Street–NY Aquarium

The New York Aquarium is the oldest continuously operating aquarium in the United States. The original aquarium opened in 1896 in Manhattan's Battery Park, and moved to its present oceanfront location at Coney Island in 1957. Construction of the new shark pavilion, called Ocean Wonders: Sharks! was planned for over a decade. In 2006, the Wildlife Conservation Society that runs the aquarium organized an international competition that challenged contestants to dream up a bold, iconic beacon for the Coney Island of the 21st century. In the end, the ideas suggested by the winning entries were too ambitious to be realized. As a result, the Seattle-based Portico Group, which specializes in designing zoos, aquariums, and botanical gardens was commissioned to develop a more realistic project. After several years of delays due to Hurricane Sandy, the new pavilion finally opened in 2018.

The three-story facility includes the main exhibit, about 45 sharks in several large water tanks; a café that spills onto the boardwalk in Coney Island, a roof deck, and classrooms. Clad in metal panels, three swirls define the new building. These are wrapped with a wind-responsive artwork, a continuous shimmer wall, which is an array of thousands of hinged aluminum and stainless steel "flappers" that sway in the wind and reflect and filter the sun and changing colors of the sky, evoking sparkling fish scales. This kinetic facade installation is by California-based artist Ned Kahn whose work is influenced by fluid motion and has been driven by the poetics of turbulence.

Queens
Long Island City, Sunnyside, Flushing Meadows,
Corona Park, Kew Gardens Hills

10

Hunters Point South Park — Swoosh

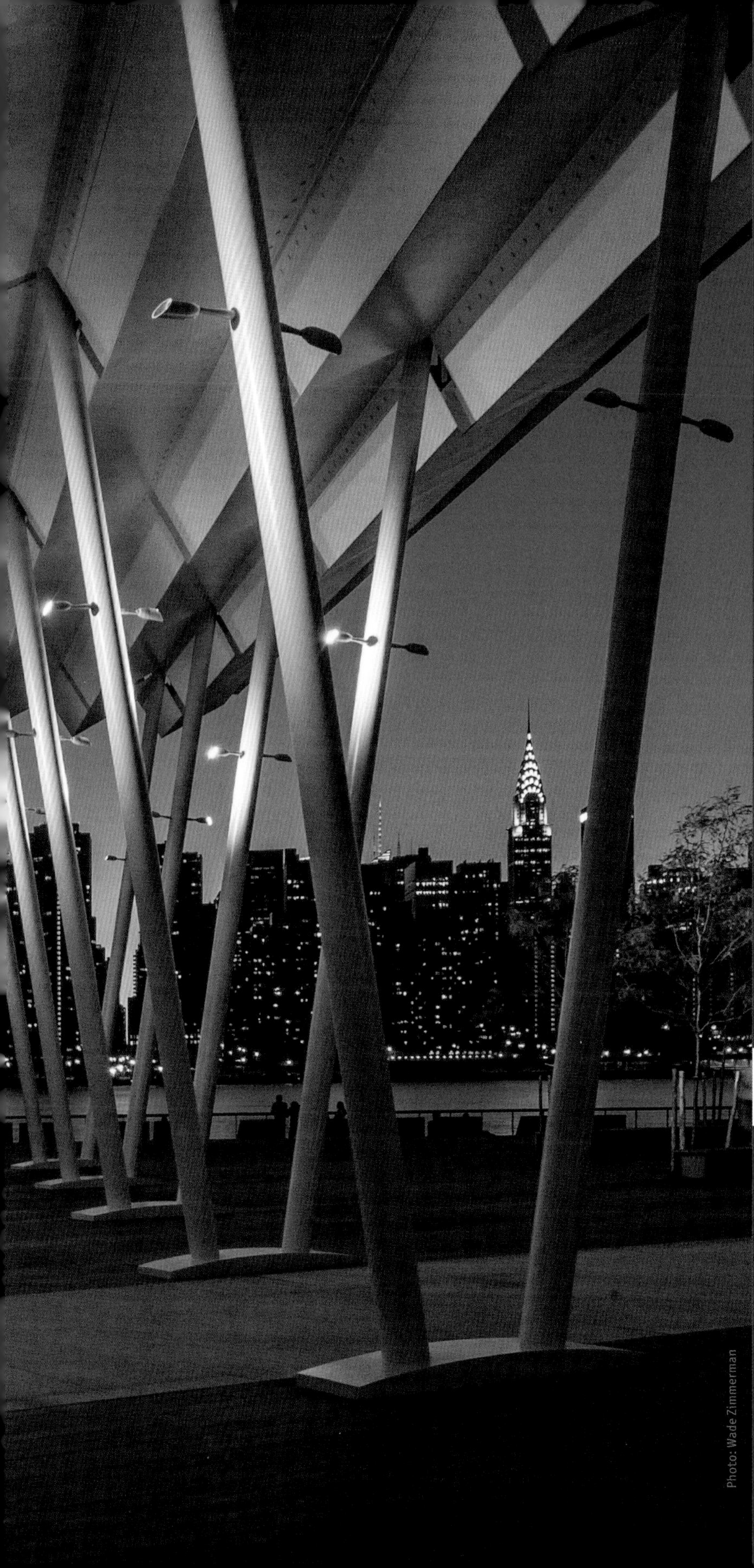

Photo: Wade Zimmerman

Photos: Albert Večerka/Esto

Hunters Point South Park—Swoosh

092 A

Hunters Point South Park,
Long Island City
*Marion Weiss and Michael
Manfredi of Weiss/Manfredi
with Thomas Balsley Associates*
2013

7 to Vernon Boulevard-Jackson Avenue
G to 21 Street
Astoria Ferry to Long Island City,
East River Ferry to Hunters Point South

Located along the East River, Hunters Point South Waterfront Park was designed by Marion Weiss and Michael Manfredi of Weiss/Manfredi. It is phase one of a larger master plan that encompasses the transformation of 30 acres (12 hectares) of post-industrial waterfront in Long Island City, the largest and westernmost neighborhood of Queens. Formerly an under-populated industrial zone, the area has seen rapid and broad gentrification, particularly due to its closeness to Manhattan's Midtown. The neighborhood is just one stop away from the Grand Central Station on subway line 7 and it offers direct automobile links to Manhattan over the Queensboro Bridge, through the Queens-Midtown Tunnel, or a quick ferry ride to East 34th Street. The park includes a picturesque, green promenade with the most gorgeous views of New York City's skyline, play and fitness areas, a dog run, a garden, a small beach, and a multi-use oval. A canopy of pleated steel, swoosh-shaped and supported on tall V-shaped tubular columns, follows the curve of the oval and offers shelter for a ferry stop and outdoor café. The park survived a four-foot (1.2-meter) surge during Hurricane Sandy in 2012, the second-costliest hurricane in the history of the United States, and acted as a protective perimeter for the surrounding community.

10

Hunters Point
Community Library — Cutouts

093 **A**

47 Center Blvd, Long Island City
Steven Holl Architects
2019

Photo: Courtesy of Steven Holl Architects

7 to Vernon Boulevard-Jackson Avenue
G to 21 Street
Astoria Ferry to Long Island City,
East River Ferry to Hunters Point South

Placed as a standalone sculpture in Gantry Plaza State Park in Long Island City, directly across the East River from the United Nations Headquarters in Manhattan, the new Hunters Point Community Library is the latest addition to the Queens Borough Public Library. Standing against the backdrop of recent generic apartment towers in this completely reinvented and gentrified neighborhood, the library, one of 62 branches in the borough, which is a separate system from both the New York City Public Library and the Brooklyn Public Library, is expected to open to the public in early 2019. The concrete structure with its attractive proportions, which its architect Steven Holl based on the golden section, is aluminum painted to give the exterior a subtle sparkle. Most notably, multi-floor, curved, glazed cutouts instead of traditional windows distinguish the building's volume. Three of them are grouped on the front east entrance side and offer peeks into the adult, teen, and kids' sections. These programmatic divisions are fluidly arranged on the inside by following a browsing path, a series of open stacks of bookshelf-flanked stairs and platforms that represent how Holl's phenomenological architecture addresses all the senses.

The library will also house offices, a cyber center, roof terrace, café, as well as an outdoor amphitheater and reading garden. The original reflecting pool next to the western facade, a common feature in Holl's poetic projects, was value-engineered out of the design, but the building comes so close to the river's edge that it will be reflected anyway. At night the glowing presence of Holl's library along the waterfront will join the historical "Pepsi Cola" sign and the old gantry crane with its massive "Long Island" signage, to become a prominent new beacon for Long Island City's revived residential community. In our 2004 interview, Holl said: "The essence of phenomenological architecture and phenomenological experience lies in the movement of the body through the space and all the phenomena that our senses can experience: the quality of light, the sound, the smell, the acoustics, and the change in the body's movement. These things are precious to architecture. Film will never take that away from architecture. Music, sculpture, and painting are all two dimensional in that sense. Architecture is one art that to experience it, is really to explore its greatest dimension, the phenomenological dimension — 100 percent."

Watercolors by Steven Holl

2222 Jackson Avenue — Pixels 094 A

2222 Jackson Avenue,
Long Island City
ODA
(Office for Design & Architecture)
2015

Ⓖ ❼ to Court Square
Ⓔ Ⓜ to Court Square-23 Street

2222 Jackson Avenue, in Long Island City, is an 11-story residential building with 175 compact rental units, located directly across the street from MoMA PS1. Designed by New York-based Israeli architect Eran Chen, this new building is based on planning strategies championed by the architect, which are in part expressed in dozens of his projects built across the city since his firm, ODA, opened in 2007. All of Chen's buildings go beyond the prototypical, extruded-box form. The architect calls his approach, "unboxing buildings." In other words, he is against the notion of reducing architecture to merely designing the facades of extruded glass boxes. It is not that extruded boxes are necessarily what the architecture of New York City looks like of late; after all, this book explores 100 iconic examples of structures that are anything but boxes. Still, armed with an expertise in zoning and building codes, ODA works within the City's byzantine regulations to uncover new and unconventional methods for maximizing voids, gaps, and both private or shared open spaces.

The architect likes to call his creations "vertical villages." As a result, 2222 literally breaks out of the box in its attempt to free itself from the familiar. The building's modular, pixelated look is achieved by stacking three types of apartments as a matrix on a modulated 12-foot (3.7-meter) structural grid: studios with one bay, one-bedrooms with two bays, and two-bedrooms with three bays. The studios are longer than their one and two-bedroom counterparts and project 7 feet (2.1 meters) beyond the facade, dancing along two sides: Jackson Avenue and Crane Street. It is this characteristic push-and-pull strategy that creates multiple corner windows and terraces for apartments above. A third of all units enjoy their spacious terraces that, according to the architect, comprise 30 percent more outdoor space than the building's entire footprint.

10

Korean Presbyterian Church — Gills

43–23 37th Avenue, Sunnyside
Douglas Garofalo, Greg Lynn, Michael McInturf
1999

7 to 40 Street-Lowery Street
M **R** to 36 Street

The Korean Presbyterian Church of New York in Sunnyside, Queens, is the result of a collaborative effort by team of three pioneers in parametric design: Douglas Garofalo (1958–2011) of Garofalo Architects in Chicago; Greg Lynn FORM in Los Angeles, then based in Hoboken, and Michael McInturf Architects in Cincinnati. The project was one of the earliest examples of the now ubiquitous parametric modeling and effective use of the computer program called Alias, developed for movie animation and industrial design. It was also an early example of a project that was built based on a digital set of construction documents. All structural elements and connections here are different. The building is literally a complex of unique parts. What it took to accomplish this project shows how quickly technology has advanced in the last 20 years. While Alias allowed the combining of novel blob elements with orthogonal geometry of the existing building to produce a complex hybrid design, the communications capacity required to exchange computer files made the design of this project too big for any of the three studios to handle it on its own. The new building is an adaptive reuse project, in which the new church structure is an addition on top of and around a 1930s laundry plant. The resulting building houses the church that hosts services for 2,500 people, a community center for the Korean American congregation, 80 classrooms, a 600-seat wedding chapel, various assembly spaces, choir rehearsal space, a cafeteria, a library, and a day care center. The original factory's industrial vocabulary is retained and its interior spaces and exterior massing are manipulated and adjusted to facilitate a unique confluence of cultural programming. The building's most notable feature is an array of gill-like metal screens dancing around the open-air exit stairs in the back of the church. These funky elements prompted Herbert Muschamp of the *New York Times* to describe the building, "as striking as those we once had to go to Los Angeles to see." When the church opened in 1999, it joined less than a handful of progressively designed buildings in the

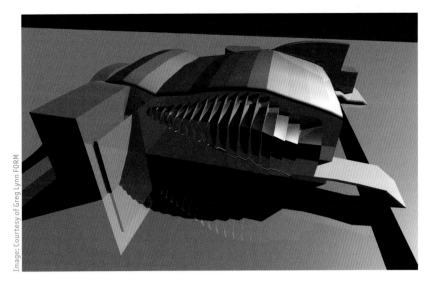

Image: Courtesy of Greg Lynn FORM

city, which signaled the emerging relevance of architecture of quality. "The church can claim a place on the small list of projects that are helping to lift New York architecture out of its long creative slump," noted Muschamp. In our 2013 interview with Gregg Pasquerelli, SHoP Architects' co-founding partner, who worked at Greg Lynn's studio at the time, shared his experience of working on the church project: "It was more like animation software that we used and we were loading parametric elements into it. It was being designed then — we were just making first steps. It was an attempt to use animation as a design tool. The building was moving and changing based on the parameters that we would put in. Then we would freeze the animation at a certain moment to try to figure out plans and sections to show how a particular form could be built. The building was designed by using an animation technique as opposed to sketching or building physical models. We never actually drew a single line; we let the animation do it. We only made decisions on when to freeze a particular view or a form when we liked what we saw."

Queens Theater in the Park — Spiral

096 A

14 United Nations Avenue South,
Flushing Meadows Corona Park
*Sara Caples and Everardo
Jefferson of Caples Jefferson Architects*
2010

7 to 111th Street

Designed by husband and wife New York-based architects Sara Caples and Everardo Jefferson of Caples Jefferson Architects, Queens Theatre in the Park is built around the ruins of the iconic New York State Pavilion for the 1964–65 New York World's Fair. The pavilion was designed by Philip Johnson and featured in such films as *The Wiz* (1978) with Diana Ross and *Men in Black* (1997) with Will Smith. The original structure is a huge open-air elliptical concert arena, futuristic observation towers, and a small low drum-like building, which was originally used as the cylindrical Theaterama about the State of New York. In 1993, the former Theaterama was converted into 476-seat community theater, designed by architect Alfredo De Vido. It was so successful that Caples Jefferson was commissioned to expand it with a 150-seat cabaret space, a large reception hall for 600 people, multifunction spaces, and offices. The theater building was conceived as a spatial experience through the use of long external ramps that generate complex spiraling forms around the circular main volume and reach their peak at the domed ceiling. While the original theater building echoes a snail, the new addition is an explicit and apt spiral. The new building is designed to give the impression that it had always been a part of the complex. Its additional elements are brought into a coherent whole by wrapping them around the original drum in a beautiful, nuanced, and surely theatrical way. The similarity in the scale and ambitions of the ruin and the new reception's pavilion are a successful dialectic — the architects created an assonance of building elements and shapes between the new and the existing structures: circular volumes, columns, and a tension-based roof are the most recognizable common features. In my conversation with the architects in 2010, Jefferson said, "We wanted the architecture to intensify visitors' experience, such as at sunset. We started with a neutral color palette in the reception space and highlighted various specific areas with sunset colors — oranges and reds — to intensify the experience of this natural phenomenon. We looked at Rothko paintings for inspiration. Part of the intensification is the uninterrupted spiral of light that reinforces the circular nature of the design, defines the vortex of circulation, and organically ties the building to the park around it."

Photo: Nic Lehoux for Caples Jefferson Architects

Kew Gardens Hills Library Expansion — Book

097 A

72–33 Vleigh Place,
Kew Gardens Hills
*Amale Andraos and Dan Wood
of WORKac*
2017

E **F**

to Briarwood then **buses Q20A** or **Q20B**

The Kew Gardens Hills Library in Flushing is a replacement and expansion of the 1966 Lindsey Library. Beirut-born Amale Andraos and her husband Rhode Island-born Dan Wood, the founders of WORKac, designed the new freestanding, single-story building. From the street it evokes a giant open book lying on its back. The library, surrounded by two- and three-story houses, is organized around the central reading room with open areas for adults, teens, children, and staff lined up along two main facades. This L-shaped zone is capped with a green roof that's visible from the street. The curtain-like facades are made of glass-fiber-reinforced concrete panels (GFRC). They are lifted up to form extensive triangular sections of clear glass. The entrance awning is articulated by folding a section of the GFRC facade over the street like a bookmark. In my 2015 interview with Andraos and Wood at their New York studio, Andraos said: "Our work is about exploring the alternative ways for cities to grow. How can so many people live in concrete and glass? I think we absolutely have to integrate nature into our lives, perhaps a constructed nature, but nature, nevertheless. We tend to do work that is quite legible and accessible, rather than focusing on performance, per se. For example, if we are concerned about collecting the rainwater then we emphasize that by sloping the roof. So, there is a kind of immediacy about understanding various systems. Nothing is hidden; everything is part of the experience of understanding the building in front of you."

10

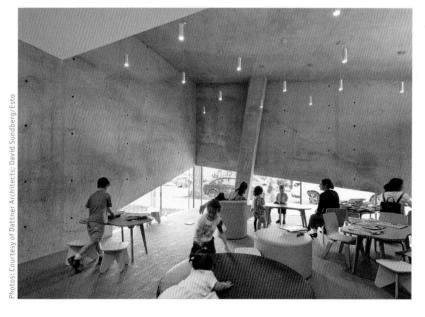

Photos: Courtesy of Dattner Architects; David Sundberg/Esto

The Bronx

Melrose, Concourse, Pelham Parkway

Via Verde—Snake
700 Brook Avenue, Melrose,
South Bronx
Grimshaw with Dattner Architects
2012

2 5 to 3 Avenue-149 Street

Situated on Brook Avenue near East 156th Street in the South Bronx, Via Verde, an affordable, sustainable residential development, shares its large block with the Bronxchester Houses, a high-rise public housing project, the University Heights High School, and a post office. The New York office of London-based Grimshaw architects designed the project, which was the winning entry in the New Housing New York Legacy Competition. The complex reflects a public commitment to the creation of the next generation of social housing. There are 222 apartments ranging from affordable rentals to middle-income coops arranged in three distinctive building types — a 20-story tower at the north end of the site, a 6- to 13-story mid-rise duplex apartment block, and two- to four-story townhouses to the south, all grouped around a series of community gardens in the center. They begin at a ground level courtyard and spiral upwards through a series of south-facing roof gardens, creating a snake-shaped promenade for residents. The ground floor features retail, a community health center, and live-work units. In my 2017 interview with Vincent Chang, Grimshaw's managing partner and the founder of the firm's New York office in 2001, the architect told me the following about the Via Verde project, which he oversaw: "It is an important model for other housing projects in the city, not as a built form but as a process, which includes the way the competition was organized by the city, and how private and public initiatives and

organizations came together in the process. The initial idea of Jonathan Rose, the project's developer, was to try to find a new interpretation between a garden and city. Despite the fact that there are multiple forms of ownership within this complex," he continued, "it was important to us to make it feel like it was a single, inclusive building. We created a whole series of ascending green terraces with apartments opening directly onto these broad gardens at various levels. They also establish a strong visual connection with Manhattan that appears to be quite close, which is important for residents to feel that they are a part of the city. We asked questions like, how to harmoniously put 200 units on a constrained site and provide fresh air, good day-lighting, views, and a place to meet. We tried to understand how the prospective tenants and owners would wish to live and what their needs were. Also, because the building's area is in transition, we imagined various possibilities for different units to grow and adapt to provide flexibility for the residents' families."

Photos: Courtesy of Dattner Architects; David Sundberg/Esto

11

Bronx County Hall of Justice — **099** **A**
Accordion
265 East 161st Street,
Concourse
Rafael Viñoly of Viñoly Architects
2007

B **D** **4** to 161 Street-Yankee Stadium

I remember working for a full year on the Bronx County Hall of Justice project as a young architect in Rafael Viñoly's office. On scheme after scheme, Viñoly turned and swapped half a dozen pedestrian bridges diagonally to connect the two blocks of the L-shaped building at various points. Eventually, they were all value-engineered out, and replaced with more economical stairs. Nevertheless, these run along the facades on the plaza side effectively, displaying the building's complex circulation patterns. As built, this 15-years-in-the-making complex stands prominently on its two-block site, facing East 161st Street, near the borough's Grand Concourse. The building's main facade expresses the judicial system's openness and transparency through a translucent accordion-fold curtain wall composed of fritted glass that allows daylight to permeate deep within the building, and screens the private circulation corridors.

Among the design features of note on this facade are the light shelves that are inserted into the glass folds; they reflect daylight to reduce heat and glare inside the building. Its diffused glazing renders effectively interiors as opaque from the outside, while providing exterior views from within. Generous slab-to-slab heights of 18 feet (5.5 meters) ensure that the courtrooms possess an authoritative sense of scale. During our 2007 interview at his New York studio, Viñoly said: "I like to compare tall buildings to bridges, because to me they represent infrastructure and a way of inventing a new type of accessible public space. They are public structures. Imagine bridges and terraces in the sky! It is so essential in our cities to celebrate bird's-eye views. It is such a memorable, unique, and absolutely essential experience in the 21st-century metropolis."

Public Safety Answering Center — Slits

100 A

350 Marconi Street,
Pelham Parkway
Skidmore, Owings & Merrill (SOM)
2016

4

to Westchester Square-East Tremont Ave,
then *bus Bx24*

The Public Safety Answering Center II (PSAC II), is a new facility that sits on a prominent site at the intersection of the Bronx and Pelham Parkway and the Hutchinson River Parkway. It was built to enhance New York City's 911 emergency-response systems, and to bring together multiple city agencies — the Police Department, the Fire Department, and Emergency Medical Services — and serve as a model for interagency cooperation. Designed by the New York office of SOM, the center was conceived as a perfect cube with very few windows due to security concerns. To mitigate the building's potentially monolithic appearance, the architects came up with a clever way of applying a serrated pattern for the facade. It is made of recycled aluminum, punched with a series of irregularly placed, tall narrow windows. The result is simultaneously sleek and anonymous. Although the openings do stand out and make a strong impression, automobile passengers on adjacent highways can catch their edgy appearance for only a few seconds. These thin windows appropriately recall arrow slits, narrow vertical apertures in medieval castles. The building is wrapped with a sculptural berm of native wild grasses that serve as a barrier to protect this modern-day fortress.

11

Featured Architects

Digits indicate project numbers

Via Verde.
Grimshaw with Dattner Architects, 2012

Photo: Courtesy of Dattner Architects; David Sundberg/Esto

Author

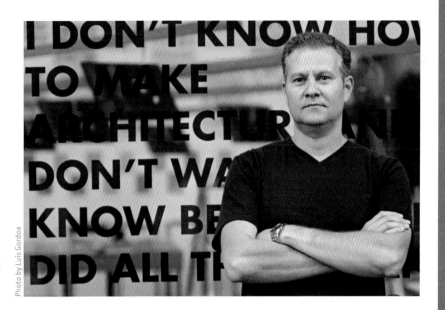

Photo by Luis Gordoa

Vladimir Belogolovsky

Vladimir Belogolovsky was born in Odessa, Ukraine, in 1970. He has lived in New York City since 1989, where he graduated from The Cooper Union School of Architecture in 1996. He has collaborated with a dozen New York architectural practices, including the offices of Rafael Viñoly, David Rockwell, and Gensler. In 2008, he founded the New York-based Intercontinental Curatorial Project, which focuses on curating and designing architectural exhibitions worldwide. Belogolovsky is the American correspondent for the architectural journal *SPEECH* (Berlin). He runs interview columns on ArchDaily.com, ArchNewsNow.com, and Archi.ru, and is a corresponding member of the International Academy of Architecture in Moscow (IAAM). His books include *Harry Seidler: The Exhibition* (Oscar Riera Ojeda Publishers, 2017); *Conversations with Peter Eisenman: The Evolution of Architectural Style* (DOM, 2016); *Conversations with Architects in the Age of Celebrity* (DOM, 2015); *Harry Seidler: LIFEWORK* (Rizzoli, 2014); and *Soviet Modernism: 1955–1985* (TATLIN, 2010).

He has written about New York for the Great Russian Encyclopedia, and has lectured widely about New York's architecture and planning principles.

Belogolovsky has interviewed many New York architects and shown their work in his numerous exhibitions, including: *Emilio Ambasz: Architecture Toward Nature* (world tour since 2017); *Architects' Voices and Visions* (Sydney, Chicago, 2016; Mexico City, Buenos Aires, 2017); *New York: Grid City* (Moscow, 2014); *Green House* at the Manezh Central Exhibition Hall (Moscow, 2009); and *Chess Game* at the Russian Pavilion (Foreign Section) at the 11th Venice Architecture Biennale (Venice, Italy, 2008). He has lectured at Columbia University, Illinois Institute of Technology, University of Virginia, UNAM in Mexico City, Hong Kong University, Moscow Architectural Institute, University of New South Wales in Sydney, Urban Redevelopment Authority in Singapore, Tongji University in Shanghai, Tsinghua University in Beijing, and other universities and museums in more than 30 countries.

The *Deutsche Nationalbibliothek*
lists this publication in the
Deutsche Nationalbibliografie;
detailed bibliographic data
are available online at
http://dnb.d-nb.de.

ISBN 978-3-86922-431-2

© 2019 by DOM publishers, Berlin
www.dom-publishers.com

*Special thanks to
photographer*
Alex Fradkin

Editor
Charles Linn

Proofreading
Amy Visram

Design
Igor Son

Maps
Katrin Soschinski

QR-codes
Christoph Gößmann

Printing
UAB BALTO print, Vilnius
www. baltoprint.lt